My 10 Years as a Middle Distance Runner--a 1000 Yard Run World Record 1969

And Other Stuff

Now 2018 Then 1968

Ralph Schultz

ISBN NUMBER 978-0-578-47559-2

BIOGRAPHY

I was born and lived on Chicago's South Side from 1947-57 and then in went to Northwestern University in Evanston, Illinois and graduated with an honors degree in history. I received a Master of Business degree from The University of Chicago in 1972. I worked for 35 years in the corporate bond business and as a loan officer in structured finance for major banks including as a vice-president for Deutsche Bank, a major German bank. In 2003 I began a new career as a college teacher and taught business courses at tribal colleges from 2005-2009 at the Pine Ridge Indian Reservation in South Dakota and the Navajo Reservation in Arizona. Sine 2009 I have taught economics at Central New Mexico Community College. In 1968 I went to Moscow Russia, the Soviet Union, to study Russian language and culture with a USA college group. I was a strategic intelligence analyst in the US Army. I was Athlete of The Year in 1969 and in 2011 was inducted into the Northwestern Athletic Hall of Fame. This book is meant to share my unique ideas about middle-distance track and field performance training and some comments about Russian history and policy today and the US economy from 1950-1965.

How I trained in 1969 to tie a World Record in the 1000 yard run and how it can help you to perform better today

What is was like growing up on the South Side of Chicago in 1947-1965.

My story-10 years of racing and my personal thoughts of life, society, and running

Outstanding Black and White Athletes

My trip to Russia in 1968 and some thoughts about Russia today and the US Economy

Email: NewMexcoach@gmail.com

RUSSIA 1968

Me and Russian schoolchildren and teacher outside Leningrad 1968: NOTE sandy ground near Finnish Gulf. So friendly and peaceful, America and the USSR.

TABLE of CONTENTS

THE STORY----SECTIONS

NOTE: I did my own editing which was a long arduous process. You may see a few imperfections and inconsistencies which would not be present if edited by a professional or a major book publisher.I did not have the resources to do this. I wrote this book over my card table and on my couch. Hey, I am imperfect and so are people and the world. I think the book works, is attractive, and very readable with many great photos. And I am honest about myself and my thoughts, beliefs. So read and enjoy! Learn. It took 3 ½ years to write this book and its two sister books, a total of 416 pages and 250 photographs. The second is about foreign policy conflicts between the USA and China and Russia and current USA economic issues. The third is about the 10 years I lived with the Lakota Sioux Indians during 1996-2008. The book is more striking in beautiful color and I may reissue all three books in one volume in color.

PREFACE

I wrote this book because I wanted to express my ideas about running in a system that worked so well for me my senior year at Northwestern University. It's all in here with my commentary, ideas, and I talk to you in a straightforward and folksy way. It's based on what worked for me when I tied a world record of 2:06 in the 1,000-yard run, that was held by Peter Snell of New Zealand. I did very well in many races at the 880 and ran a 4:06 mile my senior year at Northwestern. I think there is a lot to be learned here, and it's probably somewhat contrary to today's training. It's not meant to replace training for the star-studded national caliber athletes, nor to take the place or be competitive with today's coaching methods at collegiate or track club level. It's meant to be a book for the runner who needs some help, who is either isolated or is not part of a major program. I think it works. You can become a highly ranked athlete. And I hope you enjoy reading this and my story and my anecdotes about society. Take care of yourself and good luck.

I also have written a substantial portion about ideas that matter to me and I want to express to many people. I have a lifelong wealth of wisdom and teach economics at a community college. I also traveled to Russia/Soviet Union in 1968. It made a major impression on me. I think athletes can and should speak out on issues that they think are important. This is expressed in this book and in more detail in another to be published soon.

READERS NOTES:

What do you want to learn from this book?

Me in High School 1964

ACKNOWLEDGEMENTS

I would also like to thank Merrilyn Sweet, my good friend and high school classmate, who voluntarily assisted me to put together the photographs, transcribe my oral recordings and helped with the computer, which I have to admit is difficult for me at times. Merrilyn and I met three years ago at a high school reunion, and we have become good friends. She lives in the Chicago Metropolitan area in Riverside a beautiful suburb with many parks and trees and well maintained older classical homes. And two designed by Frank Lloyd Wright, the famous architect. Thank you Merrilyn.

And to Blaine, my 29-year-old son. Thank you for helping me managing photographs and getting it published and marketed on social media.

Kurt Tyler also was invaluable providing technical publishing advice. He is the author of two recently self-published books.

Below: 1st mile 4.09.5 @ Northwestern. Final 440 in 56.

Some of you may still not understand why an athlete writing about their running experience would make commentaries about world issues. Because it is who I am. Athletes are multifaceted and can offer their insights that will be respected and challenge another person's ideas and provide food for thought to consider and ponder. We need not always listen to experts, politicians, and news people.

So the period I mostly write about, 1962-72 was a time of intense social, political and economic change in the United States. And it was actually a very exciting time to live. And there was so much change going on and other ideas and ways of living to consider.

So come along and share my journey and have a good read.

Ralph Schultz December 30, 2018

THE BOOK

This book is primarily for you, the aspiring experienced middle-distance runner who still wants to compete and improve your performance and achieve your goals and dreams. it is how you can train like I did at age 21 in 1969 in the 1000 yard run and set a world record and also about life growing up on the south side of Chicago in a Polish and Ukrainian neighborhood in the 1950's, and how IT SHAPED MY RUNNING CAREER.

I am dedicating this book to a kinder gentler world.

MY ACCOMPLISHMENTS IN TRACK

Chicago Tribune

SUNDAY, MARCH 2, 1969

SPORTS 2

BUSINESS 4

N. U.'S SCHULTZ TIES WORLD RECORD

TAKES 1,000 WITH 2:06 IN BIG TEN TRACK MEET

Mantle Retires from Baseball at 37

Arrington Leads Wisconsin to Team Title

OHIO DEFEATED BY NOTRE DAME

Hirsch's View of Nickname: 'Crazy, Man'

SHAW, AARON 1ST AT DORAL, BUT HERE COMES NICKLAUS

Today's Events in Chicago

DOC REISER OPERATING ON CUB 'ANEMIA'

YANK SUPER-STAR HIT 536 HOMERS IN 18-YEAR CAREER

Most Valuable in A. L. Three Times

Fast-Stepping Wildcat

RIGHT FIELD? IT'S BUDDY'S

Bradford Sparkles in Sox Drills

CHICAGO TRIBUNE, SUNDAY, MARCH 2, 1969

SCHULTZ TIES SNELL'S WORLD 1,000 RECORD

The Summaries

College Basketball

'Composite Man'

Exhibition Baseball

Big Ten Standings

Mickey's N...

Knox Family, Sports Star

March 1969 Chicago Tribune

Yes, I had quite a 10-year life as a star track athlete. Not one of the super best in the world, but close. Sixth ranked in the USA in high school (secondary school) in 1965 (1:51.9 800 meters). Third in the National Collegiate Athletic Association (NCAA) outdoor 880 in 1968 and All American. Big 10 Outdoor 880 Champion in 1967 and 1000 yard run Indoor Champion in 1968, 1969, Olympic tryout finalist 1968. Member of the 1970 and 1971 UCTC (University of Chicago Track Club coached by the highly regarded Ted Haydon) 2 Mile Relay teams that won the Indoor National Amateur Athletic Union (NAAU) Meet twice at Madison Square Garden in New York City on national television and many other first-place finishes. Tied the World Indoor 1000 yard record in 1969 held by Peter Snell of New Zealand (2:06). My best 800-meter time was 1:46.6 in 1969, 14th in the world, and tied with a Kenyan. I ran on a USA track team in Europe in 1970. I had the thrill to meet several all-time great athletes. When in high school I met and was interviewed by the great American sprinter Jesse Owens for a trip to the 1964 Olympic games as a good will ambassador to the Russian team. I was learning Russian in high school. I got to know Willie White, a FIVE-time woman Olympic long jumper at The University of Chicago Track Club meets, and on a USA track team sent to Europe to compete internationally. I had dinner with the Highland Park High School (Illinois, North Shore) track coaches in 2005. Rick Wohlhuter and Peter Snell sat next to me, both Olympic stars and 800 meter run world record holders. In 2011 I was inducted into the Northwestern University Athletic Hall of Fame, quite an honor. In 1969 I was awarded the Big 10 Medal of Honor. Only one is given at each Big 10 school to one athlete out of ALL the varsity sports. What a long way I had come since Evergreen Park High school. How did all this happen, to an ethnic Polish-German kid from the south side of Chicago?

ME

All right. This is Ralph Schultz. It's July 16, 2015 (this is when I began to write). I'm going to record a story about my life in track for ten years and with some side anecdotes about my life and what I believe in. (like America in the 1950's and 1960's, what I call the economic SURGE, that carried us along into a burgeoning America which I discuss later). My story is intended for people of all ages whether runners or not, but primarily for current competitive middle-distance runners, whom I hope to inspire to train the way I did to get that maximum performance without injury. It is for runners age eighteen to thirty, perhaps some who have never quite reached their potential, just out of college, or runners who don't have the time to train like they used to, perhaps they're in graduate school or they've become part of the working force, or teachers, or have a college coach with no middle-distance experience, but they still want to perform at a high level. I'd like to help runners, who are perhaps a 4:10 miler trying to break 4:00, or 1:52 half-miler trying to break 1:48 and get to a national level, a higher level, as I did. Or a 4:20 miler to a 4:10. But any runner of any age and ability level can benefit. So my story is an interesting one. I hope you enjoy it, and I hope this word gets spread all over the world.

THE BEGINNING:

Track started officially in the spring of 1962, my freshman year in high school (secondary 9-12) in March. But it actually started when I was a little boy, age eight or nine. I went to a YMCA 2-week summer camp, Camp Hastings, on a lake in the far northern suburbs of Chicago. Incredibly in 1990 my wife and I bought a house in a development right next to the camp, 33 years later. How ironic is that! You see, I lived in Chicago on the South Side, which I'm very proud of, in an area called Back of the Yards, at 55th Street (or Garfield Blvd.) and Ashland, about four miles west of The University of Chicago and about eight miles southwest of Downtown Chicago. More on that to come.

Chicago

A beautiful Lakefront. 3 million people and 9 million in the entire metropolitan area.

Named the "City with Broad Shoulders" by the famous author Carl Sandberg

US Steel

Growing up I remember the smell of gasoline fumes blowing in from the massive oil refineries in nearby Indiana. I liked it and to me it was a clean good smell, and a reminder of the industrial power around Chicago. I also liked to drive over the big bridge by Lake Calumet Port with my parents and look in wonder at the massive industrial plants on the Indiana-Illinois border and all the ships carrying grain from Midwest farms. I still do. It was exciting and indicative of a strong secure city and country without all the self-doubts of today. We also burned coal for heating in this large cast iron furnace in the basement. I helped my Grandpops shovel the coal pellets from the coal bin into the burning furnace and empty the large embers called clinkers with a big pair of tongs. I liked the odor, the deep black color, and the texture of the coal too. Things were really different then.

GRANDPOPS JOE GORECKI 1952

ME-Mom kept me well groomed

My mother sent me to camp to become more independent. I never learned to swim because I spent a lot of time in the lake marsh with my friends hiding from each other on trails through cattails and doing other adventures and not going to camp activities. At the end of camp we had the minnow race (little fish) the last day of camp at the small beach with a dock there. We wore an inner-tube, and we raced out to the end of the dock, oh, I would guess about sixty feet the distance from home plate to the pitcher's mound and back. And I took off, lunging through the water, pushing as hard as I could because it went up to my chest with this inner-tube around me, and I lunged and pushed back to the beach and I won the race. I got a Clark candy bar and some applause. I remember charging towards the beach thrilled that I was in front as I saw the sandy beach getting nearer. I had the same feeling when I charged down the final 70 yards and set the World Record. Nothing would stop me! So I guess that's when it really started, the racing ability and determination. Through my childhood, I was very, very active. We played football in the fall. Basketball wasn't popular then. And baseball all spring, summer and early fall. I was both a New York Yankees and Cubs fan. But the White Sox were good too. They won the American league pennant in 1959. I can still recite their starting lineup. And oh how I looked up to Mickey Mantle, the Yankees super star and slugger. And occasionally, we had races and played kick the can (a mix of "It" and "Hide and Go Seek"). I could go on this story forever, but I had a great, friendly group of friends, buddies. We called it a gang then, a harmless type, who hung out together and played and were very active on bikes and energetic (we also played a lot of board games in the winter). I always had a lot of endurance. We stuck together. And played marbles. Remember that game?

Saturday was the day we all went on long excursions to "other unexplored neighborhoods" on bike or by foot. It took all afternoon, some of these places were only ½ mile away, others 2 miles. But if they were the other side of a city barrier, like a busy boulevard, park, through a viaduct, or a strange commercial shopping district, we were on alert for new excitement, people, even danger, so we imagined. We even played hopscotch, drove our red wagons all over on chalk highways we outlined all around our block. We all lived on "blocks". How about trading baseball cards, I had a big impressive collection. In winter we had a few favorite small sledding hills on vacant lots, but we liked it and sled down from 4-5 PM under grey 29-degree days. Then home for some hot chocolate. And I recall at 5 PM I had to run inside to watch a TV kids show called Gumby. Loved it. He is still around. Gumby is this flexible rubbery clay like animated cartoon figure that got into all sorts of adventures. And a favorite board game was Clue. At age 11 it changed to Careers and Avalon Hill complex war games like Gettysburg. I was always a civil war buff. I read many books about it and still do. You have to read Killer Angels about the Battle of Gettysburg from the viewpoint of the South. In 8th grade I belonged to the Civil War Roundtable.

Funny thing, we lived 4 miles due west from The University of Chicago. Little did I know that the amateur track program there would enhance my running career 10 years later! I would also attend The University of Chicago Graduate Business School, earning an MBA in finance. I am very proud of graduating from The University of Chicago, one of the best universities in the world, a bastion and center of intellectual thought and creativity.

We moved to Evergreen Park in 1957, a southwest side suburb next to Chicago. It had just sprung up from a small somewhat rural looking town during the burgeoning US housing boom of the 1950's. The high school was built in 1956. Most of the student's parents had moved from the south side of Chicago ethnic neighborhoods (where they had lived with their parents in older homes and apartments) to new modest homes, a step up in living standards. It was really a mass migration to a new opportunity and a better life. Part of the American Dream for sure. My step-father was the only one of my parent's relatives or friends who had a college degree, a Bachelor of Science in Business Administration from DePaul University in Chicago. It was paid for by the G.I. Bill, a huge new government subsidy for WWII veterans. Big government at its best. These young people were part of the of the newly educated that went to build America during the post WWII Surge and greatly improve the standard of living. In 1938 only 6% of the population over 25 years of age were college graduates, in 1969 16%, and today 33%. The GI Bill also provided vocational training. By 1956 nine million veterans had used the bill, three million for college and six million for job training.

My parent's friends were all working men's families, a plumber, iron worker, Brinks Security long distance driver, car salesman, mailman, brick layer, garbage sanitary collector, butcher, electrician, machinist, restaurant owner, insurance salesman, a small clothing store owner, a bowling alley entrepreneur, a government office bureaucrat for the Veterans Administration, and two Chicago Police Officers, one, named Peter, a Lt. Detective assigned to the Vice Squad, with a white flattop haircut, the other, Johnnie, who drove a police squad car. All the moms stayed home and took care of the family and house, a very important nurturing big job. All part of a new growing middle-class America. I had a childhood that was normal on the outside, a basketball hoop on the garage, a home in a southwest suburban modest middle-class neighborhood adjacent to Chicago-Beverly (where the rich people lived). I played on 10-foot high dirt piles and ran through prairies on paths we made in weeds up to my shoulders, played army and had hobbies, made toy ships and planes, and again was very active. During the summer I played in baseball youth leagues, ages 9-13. It was a summer ritual-I loved it. Played third base, an excellent fielder, pitcher, and steady line drive hitter. We won a few championships too. What else but baseball in 1959? After some of the games at 8 PM the parents and some of us players went to the American Legion Hall for hot dogs, cokes, and we played arcade bowling with automatic pop up pins and a round metal disc we slid at the pins.

Age 13 Summer League Baseball

I started playing basketball in 7th and 8th grade at Central Junior High School, all new to me. I had fun making long looping shots and racing down the court. I was also in the Boy Scouts at age 12 and one wintry cold morning the entire troop went on an outing to a small lake and we ice-skated around a small island. Around and around. I just took off, skating furiously, passing everyone, loop after loop around the island, for almost an hour, sweating like a horse. Endurance I was born with for sure, and passion. Recently I visited it and memories came flooding back (August 2016). Then I ran/walked 2 miles in the Palos forest preserves where I had trained 40 years ago and the deep green forest. I still enjoyed sweating, running.

READERS NOTES: What was your childhood favorite sport? Why?

The island I skated around in 1960 over and over-and me in 2017-

Super G TWA Constellation

In 1958 my mother and I flew to Los Angeles, California, from Chicago out of Midway Airport to visit family and friends. What an adventure! That was the end of the propeller aircraft era just before the jets arrived. Going out we were on a TWA Super G Constellation, just a beautiful elegant plane with the three tails. Remember? It was classy, roomy seats, great food on real plates and silverware, attentive stewardesses (old word before feminism), all women then. Everyone nicely dressed. We returned on American Airlines on a DC-7, the workhorse of passenger planes. It was all metallic silver with the red and blue American color emblem on the tail and side. Both aircraft had four propeller engines and flew at one-half the speed of today's jets. Three hours now versus seven hours then. But the time passed ok.

And they flew at only at 20,000 feet, not 35,000 as today. And there were many more airlines then, before deregulation of the industry put many out of business. At Midway there were many airlines at the small terminal. Sometimes I try to remember them all. Let's see. United, American, TWA, Eastern, Southern, Western, Braniff, Mohawk, Allegheny, North Central, Delta, Northwest, Continental, Lake Central, National, Northeast, Ozark, Pan Am, Piedmont. We went to the tower to the Observation Deck to watch takeoffs. Great fun, exciting. But all these amenities and luxury were paid for by higher airfares. Adjusted for inflation round trip was $1,450 Chicago to Los Angeles, today $500. LA was just developing then. We took a city bus from Downey where we were staying to Anaheim and Disneyland. It had been open only 2 years. And guess what the entire place was surrounded by orange groves still, not a crowed urban commercial cityscape like now. I remember the jungle boat ride, and running all over Tom Sawyers Island, a maze of winding trails, hidden nooks, and caves. Loved it! My imagination went wild!

We also went to Long Beach at the southern edge of Los Angeles for 2 days. The beach had clumps of gooey oil scattered around, blown in from the offshore oil rigs about ½ mile off the beach. I had fun anyway, playing in the sand and ocean waves.

Comiskey Park Chicago White Sox

Hey Sox fans can you recite the Chicago White Sox starting lineup in the 1959 World Series? Here goes. 1st base Ted Kluzewski (Klu), 2nd base Nellie Fox, 3rd Bubba Phillips, Shortstop Louis Aparicio, Center Field Jim Landis, Right field Jim Rivera, Left Al Smith, Catcher Sherman Lollar, pitchers Early Wynn knuckleballer, Billy Pierce a class person and starter, Turk Lown in relief. The great outfielder, Minnie Minoso was injured and out for the Series. A real White Sox hero All Star, (born in Cuba). Remember the rawhide odor of the baseball gloves? And we used wooden bats, such a solid sounding hit. I recall walking to the sporting goods store and spending a long time looking at the gloves and trying out different baseball bats that just felt right. I also went to the library a lot when I was a kid. From ages 6-10 my mom drove me to the Chicago Sherman Park library after school when I browsed around and read all the books about dinosaurs and geography. From ages 10 to 13 after we moved to the suburbs, I remember walking to the local little library. It was like the size of a small shop maybe six times the size of a two- car suburban garage. I checked out books on sports stars, geography, history, and some adventure stories. I walked a mile one way to get there. Reading helps you think. I was always very curious, "why, why, why?" I always asked. My parents called me the "why" kid. Not to brag but 7 years ago I took the reading section of the college ACT exam, since I was going to be a test tutor. I almost fainted. I scored a 34, 99th percentile-that's 99%. I'm just sayin. During this time I read, read, read. That year, out of work, I read 25 books. The mind is like a muscle, the more you work it, the stronger it gets. Remember that.

However, growing up, my father left town when I was eight. It really severely wounded me. And my mother had remarried when I was four because she was divorced when I was one, to a man who had a really good side but also a really dark side of domestic violence. And he terrified me, caused me problems for most of my life. He yelled and threatened me until he died in 2000 from a massive heart attack. Frankly I was relieved. Free at last. I had stress most of my life until about 12 years ago when years of psychotherapy finally brought me some healing. I had terror primal screaming dreams often and woke up the barracks at 3 AM when in the Army. They are mostly gone now. I suffered through a few severe bouts of depression. Today at age 70 I still am a little anxious and insecure, and lack some confidence, and worry too much. The strange part is this motivated me because, as I got older, particularly into the competitive world of sports in high school, I was desperate to prove myself worthy and excel. And I excelled in sports and I excelled in school. So in a way, I have to take my hat off to John. That's the irony of life, I guess.

But we also played chess together, baseball, fishing, and our family took road trips all over the Midwest on his business trips. He also gave me those Air Force boots I ran in during the winter snow.

Father and me in 1984 Richard Schultz

But anyway, thank goodness I loved my birthfather and have fond memories of him taking us places, despite his early exit from my life. He was an American POW (prisoner of war) at The Battle of the Bulge in 1944 in Europe and was in a German Stalag or prison camp. The guards gave him cigarettes since he was German. But he was malnourished and lost a few teeth. My step-father, John, was in Italy during WWII and hit by artillery shrapnel twice. He said you get used to artillery bombardment. Eventually he was assigned to be an aide for a General, a safe behind the lines assignment. He brought back a German Luger pistol he showed me.

SUMMER JOBS--I hated every job I had as a youth. I was a paper delivery boy as a youth in 6th, 7th grade. After school a batch of afternoon newspapers were dropped off at my home. The Chicago American and The Daily News. Both are no longer in business. I rolled them and took off on my Schwin big tire bike through the neighborhood and threw them on the front porch of houses as I pedaled by. Sometimes I hit the screen door, boom! and the resident came out and yelled at me. I had a short stint as golf caddy at Ridge Country Club. Summer, 1964, I was 16, and worked as a busboy at my step-Dads' cousin's supper club, The Red Lantern Inn. Long late hours, never stopped moving clearing and setting tables, waitresses pushing me to go go go. Summer 1965 Data Analyst on Motorola color picture tube experimental factory assembly line. Sat on a stool and took oven temperature. Summer 1966 Wildcat

Club camp counselor for 10-12 year olds. Summer 1967 Liquor store stockman. Summer 1969 small Italian grocery store, stocked shelves, cashier. See what I mean. Torture.

Anyway, to get back to the athletic side of things, I played high school football in the fall of 1962. And my goodness we had to work our tails off, double workouts in the heat. We weren't allowed to drink water in those days. Is that crazy? At the end of the day, we all ran, oh, I would guess, maybe a half mile. And I would be the first or second way out in front all the time because I had natural endurance, and I also pushed hard. I played halfback and defensive safety. The winter was basketball. I improved a lot by the end of the year. I was a good shooter so I played guard. The workouts for basketball were really arduous, and it helped put me in great shape. Boyhood was fading behind me.

Well, here's how it really started, and I owe my start to coach John Megson a man who I dearly loved and still do, who was the high school athletic director and also head track coach. He died about 20 years ago. I have had beautiful dreams about him still. Meggie (what we called him with warm respect) had gone to Upper Iowa University in Cedar Rapids and was a real fatherly Dutch Uncle type of personality. He smoked a pipe and wore coaches athletic clothes. He was a hurdler in college, now with short, gray thinning hair, probably age fifty then. He seemed to me to be one of the older teachers. Anyway, he spoke in a voice, which was empathetic and warm. And he was a gym teacher, so in early March we were having track as our section in gym, and we were running indoors. Of course, we had no running track like the fancy suburbs in the western part of Chicagoland. We would run through the gym, down the stairs to the locker room, through the locker room and then up the stairs again to the wrestling

Coach Megson and me at Elmwood Park Relays 1965

room, through it and down two flights of stairs for several laps. I was leading way in front. And I remember, he just stopped and pointed at me. And I'll never forget these words as long as I live. He pointed at me and said, "You, I want you out for track." And it resonated with me and I lit up like a Christmas tree. And then it was off to the races. It was a pivotal event. And all March, during the end of the basketball season and on break, I read every book on track in the library: *How To Train* by Fred Wilt. All sorts of things. *The Roger Banister Story,* how he broke the four-minute mile and a book *TNT: The Power Within You* which inspired me to be a winner like a thoroughbred racehorse. I devoured it and the inspiration propelled me into a sense of incredible determination and courage. And I took notes and was totally motivated. Jerry Post, a wrestling coach, said I was the most determined athlete he had ever seen.

So I went out for track and, you know, it was all new to me. And we didn't train very scientifically at that high school because it was not known for track and we didn't have the methods and understanding that the professional-like high schools did in the western and northern suburbs of Chicago. So we'd go out and run two miles, a cross-country run. I had to struggle to keep up with the varsity, but I did. And then we'd run laps around the school. It was about 660 yards or so. The workout amounted to an all-out time trial, which I was always up near the front. Not bad for a freshman. And I just killed myself. It was amazing. If I did that today I'd fall over dead. Oh, by the way, remember I'm 70, and a youthful one. But I don't run as much anymore, but still 10-15 times per month. I run two or three miles pretty slow, walk a little. But it's okay. I know it's good for me and I still enjoy it on a moderate basis. But lately I have also been running hills around the local golf course. Last summer I ran/walked 49 days in a row! I just started one day in August and kept on going, sorta like Forest Gump (Tom Hanks movie) by running around Swan Pond in beautiful Riverside, Illinois, and just kept on one day at a time, amazed I could still could do a streak like that. Ironically, I ran meets there in high school. My friend Merrillyn lives down the street. Sometimes I push it some and run for time, about 13-14 minutes per mile. Three years ago I ran an 11:17 mile on a high school track. I keep it below anaerobic level and don't push too hard. I still love running and competed in 5Ks on and off for my whole life as Ted Haydon encouraged and shaped us to do. I ran a 35:52 5K at age 63 at 5000 feet elevation. Today this world has developed a dedicated mass of seemingly semi-professional, so-called amateur weekend runners. These are the ones that don't even run for money but just learned about running later in life, and they train like crazy, eat the right stuff and buy all the latest top equipment. I find it kind of amusing, sometimes a little irritating for some strange reason. But they good people. Last year I ran 77 days in a row at age 70.

Anyway, I went on, and I ran the mile in the Spring. And I hadn't quite matured yet. Puberty was barely starting for me. And I was maybe 5'6", 130-some pounds. A little barrel-chested as I always was, and I was a little wider even when I was thin so I always looked a little like a baseball player third baseman (my position), or maybe a high school defensive safety or football running back Not a slightly built runner. It always bothered me a little, but it was part of the oxygen capacity I had I believe. So we ran lots of meets and races, two or more a week. I think it was on Tuesdays and Thursdays. The season went on, and also the tournament relays on Saturdays. The bottom line result is I finished fourth in the sophomore Southwest Suburban Conference Meet Mile. I was the fastest Freshman. I ran a 5:04.5 there, at Homewood Flossmoor High School. So it began.

My first race that freshman season in 1962 was at Blue Island High School. There was a small Clark Oil gasoline refinery next to the high school athletic fields. So much for environmental standards in those days! Only on Chicago's metropolitan south side. Strangely enough, that's where my father had gone to high school. And I think I ran about a 5.25, and I felt like I was running out in the middle of the desert, finished about third perhaps. And anyway, that was my start. Interestingly, all my German relatives are buried in a nearby Lutheran Cemetery. They have beautiful large headstones going back to birthdates in 1845-1880. My great, great grandfather was born in Prussia (the disciplined militaristic Germans) and immigrated here to the USA in the 1880's. All my male relatives have middle or first names of Christian or Christie. Mine is Christie. I like that traditional continuity. My grandfather had a Rheingold beer distributorship back in the 1950's. My father used to take me with him when he made deliveries. I loved that.

Lutheran Cemetery Blue Island Illinois

My great grandmother migrated here from Poznan Poland in 1882, a kind classy woman. I have always thought that Polish people don't have a mean bone in their bodies. I spent the summer of 1962 going to Aqua Pool Park getting a tan and hanging out. Surely I didn't train. I played terrible golf at the overcrowded Marquette Park Chicago public golf course. It was a Lithuanian neighborhood. Chicago was divided into ethnic enclaves. Pretty cool. I also ran some workouts there when I was in high school. In the fall, the varsity football coach thought I would make a good fullback. And when I didn't show up for practice, he asked me to come in to talk to him, and I was scared. But I went out for cross-country. I decided I had to focus on what I seemed to be good at. I was a pretty good baseball player. I eventually left that sport behind too. Well, we had a great cross-country team. I was on the varsity. I was about the fourth or fifth guy. We won everything. We won the Conference Meet at Homewood Flossmoor by a record large margin (low score). Then we qualified for the State Meet held at the Urbana Country Club downstate near the University of Illinois with all the great runners from the other northern and western suburbs. Evergreen Park finished way back somewhere, but we had fun and I was in awe. Maybe York won it. Who's surprised? York High School is one of the premier cross-country programs in the United States from Elmhurst, Illinois. Joe Newton was the famous coach. But he really worked those guys. Our workouts were baby stuff next to them. We had some strange workouts. We'd warm up, do some exercises. Then we'd run about a half mile, a quick jog, and then we'd form a single file and do an Indian run (my coach's words) with water in our mouth. Maybe a dozen of us, we would jog a fairly fast pace, and the guy in the back would then have to sprint to the front and spit out the water. And when he got back up there, the other guy in the behind had to sprint to the front. And occasionally, we'd have time trials. Oh, we'd run maybe a mile and a quarter hard. But we did start three-mile road runs, going out to the Palos Forest Preserves, which I truly loved. I really did. And I still do.

1963

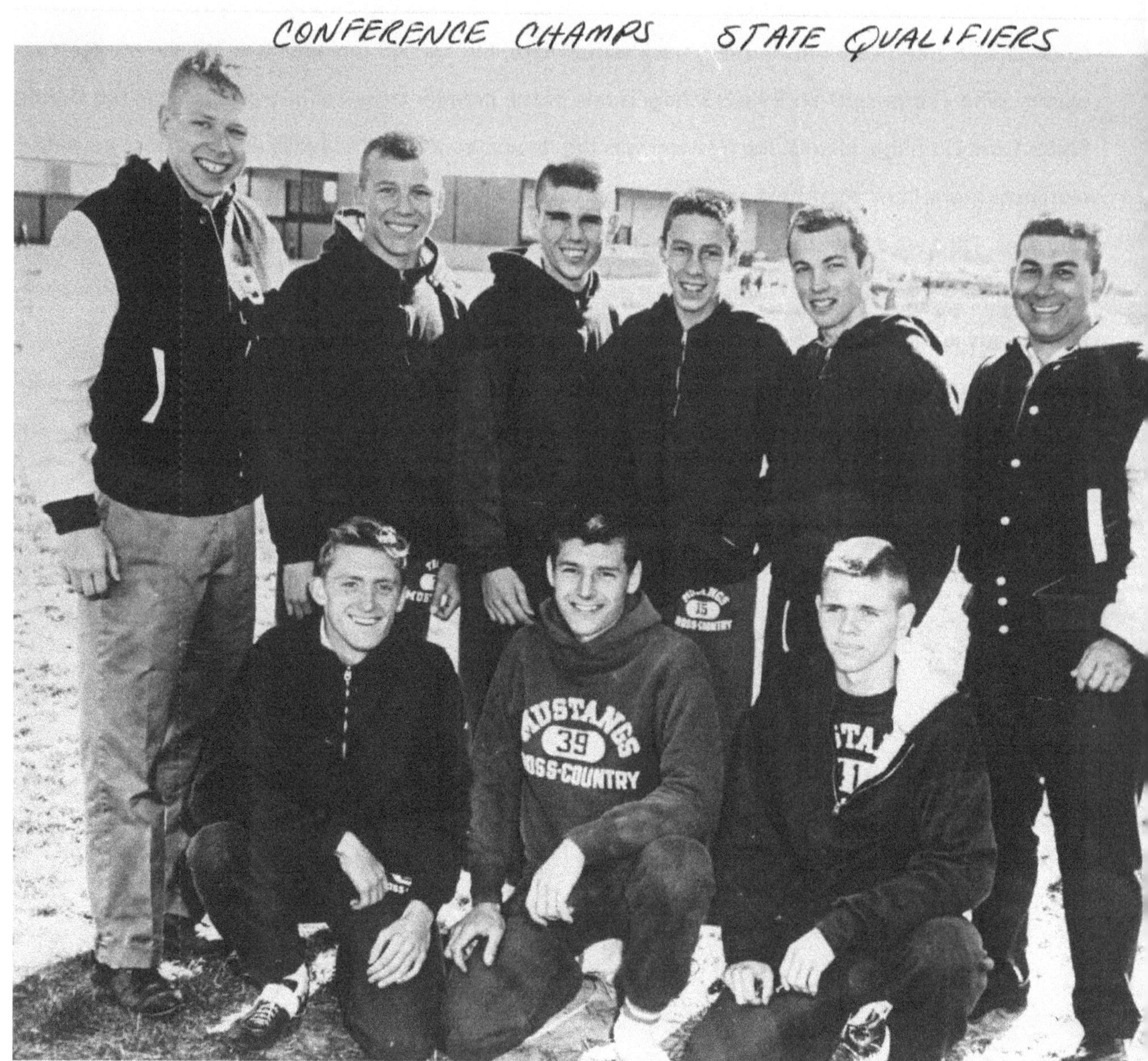

Back left to right: Assistant Coach Storbeck, Me #8 finish at Conference Meet, Pat Meehan #14, Bob Zander #5, Jim Limber #16, Coach George, Front: Alan Kloos #2, Ed Polaski #1, Bob Riley #4 -Total points 20-a long standing Conference record

PALOS FOREST PRESERVE RUNNING PATH-BEAUTY SERENE

GREEN MONSTER GOLF COURSE HILLY FAIRWAY RUNNING IN SNOW DURING WINTER

Rocky grueling uphill running on skis in Siberia Russia

EVEN STRANGER WORKOUTS: Rocky Balboa vs. DRAGO, the USSR Russian Boxer and training in the Russian wilderness. Remember Rocky IV?

Rocky training in Siberia Russia for boxing match

I also ran some weird intensive workouts in high school. They built strength and tenacity. Nothing textbook there. No official coach directed timed workouts on indoor tracks. Or outdoors paced distance runs. Oh no, not for me. You must realize I was isolated. In the southwestern suburbs of Chicago in the 1960's there were no indoor tracks, no indoor season, and no highly experienced distance running coaches. So I improvised. Just like Rocky Balboa (Sylvester Stallone).

So what really built strength and anaerobic capacity were my winter after school runs and sprints at Evergreen Park Golf Course at 93rd Street. I loved to golf there in the summer, nice and green, hilly, wooded, and some long flat areas too. So imagine the winter with 12-18-24 inches of snow on the course fairways. Remember in those days winter was constantly colder and snowier. To develop myself and stay competitive with the track boys from the elite prestigious highly coached suburban schools I ran here all by myself from 4-5 PM two or three days a week. I walked and jogged from my home to the course, about a mile through town. And I also went past one of the first McDonalds with the golden arches. And then Da Da!! There it was, my training hideaway with a blanket of snowy hills and 440-yard straightaways. I couldn't wait to run this challenging layout and improvise hard workouts. I was bundled up in layers, gloves, stocking cap, scarf, long underwear, and a WWII pair of worn US Air Force combat flight boots that must have weighed 5 pounds each. But after 20 years the leather was wrinkled and tattered. They buckled up and had rabbit fur lining for warmth. Big and bulky, about 10 inches up my leg. Emil Zatopek the great Czech distance runner and Henry Rono world record holder from Kenya also ran in military boots. That's all he had in Kenya for a while when his shoes wore out. He also was in the Kenyan army and began his running career then.

In the summer of 1971 at army basic training at Fort Ord, California I set the base mile record in combat boots in 4:52. Our Commanding Officer bought my platoon a case of beer. Proud of that I'll tell you. The army wasn't all bad. I learned that a platoon builds a tremendous brotherly democratic bond with one another. That's how the army fights, each man helping each other. Sometimes I think everyone should go through basic training. We might have a more considerate, disciplined, and humble population. I still remember those guys fondly, actually miss them.

PICTURE OF FORT ORD CA WHEN STILL AN ARMY BASE-

GUNG HO!!

FT ORD CALIFORNIA--ARMY BASIC TRAINING 1971

So off I went on the snowy golf course for 45 minutes, running long gradual hills, steep ones, up lonely sledding hills, past trees, and down those long flat 400-yard fairways all out until I collapsed at the end in the icy white snow panting like crazy. This was great! I totally ran myself out and was soaking wet with sweat. Then I walked jogged back home as it got dark ready for supper prepared by my mom.

The Actual "GREEN MONSTER"

440 YARDS OF HELL-ALL OUT RUN IN WINTER SNOW IN AIRFORCE PILOT COMBAT BOOTS (Green Fairway)

But there is more. We had lots of snow in those days before global warming. I had to shovel our 30-foot long driveway with 2 feet of snow on it. Into big mounds of snow. Yes, it was forced hard labor. Sometimes I had to do this after 2 hours of hard basketball practice until I quit the team in January 1964. But this exercise was not enough. I needed to run, so after shoveling or sometimes without needing to do it I ran on cold clear nights when I hadn't gone to the golf course. So about 8 PM I would blast-run as hard as I could dressed in winter clothes for a ½ mile down the edge of a residential street in crunchy packed snow. And I did it 4 times (back and forth twice and as hard and fast as I could with only a few minutes rest). That's 2 miles of intense paced 880-yard runs. I loved it out there in the quiet night frosty air. Then when I got back home I often went into the basement next to the furnace and turned it on full blast blowing on me and did 20 minutes of calisthenics in my heavy winter clothing. Oh yes, I really, really did. Here's another improvised killer winter workout, 2 1/2-pound Velcro wrist and ankle bands strapped to each limb. That's a total of 10 pounds. Sometimes I wore these and did 3-mile runs or intervals. Once in March, outdoors on the school parking lot, snow melting in puddles, I sprinted 50 x 50 yards, with a 15 second rest with the Velcro weights strapped to my arms and ankles. The new Athletic Director, Mr. Juska, had recently been hired from Lyons Township High School, one of those powerhouse elite western suburban schools I emulated. He praised me from his car window, in his blunt and candidly sincere way, and said he would tell my coach how hard I was training. I swelled with pride and inspiration.

Another part of my training was building overall body strength without bulk. So I did isometrics. You have a canvas belt about 6 feet long with it sewn together every 12 inches. You stand on a 3-foot-long metal bar which is holding the bottom canvas rung on the floor. You slide another metal bar into various slots and push or pull as hard as you can for 5-15 seconds. I did various types for shoulders, biceps, abdomen, ankles, and squats for legs. It was tough. I also did sit-ups with a large round metal weight behind my head. Once I did 50 sit-ups with a 25-pound weight behind my head!! The weight was like a sewer manhole cover. All these exercises built strength AND endurance.

The other thing I want to say about running is that I had a smooth stride. I've been recently watching films from high school and college, and I had the same form whether I was running the 440, 880 or mile. It's just that I ran faster and pumped my arms harder. But the basic form didn't change. Someone once said I should've been a miler, and that's how I started out. And maybe I should've been because I know I could've run a sub 4-minute mile, maybe trimmed a few pounds off. But I was built firmly, and I didn't have any fat on me. I just was a strong kid with a barrel chest. And I could run smoothly and efficiently, burn less energy, maintain stride and just keep going. And I think I was just a tad too slow for the 880/800.

Summer 2016 at my golf course winter training hideaway 50 years later. Note my enthusiasm and happiness. Rolling hills in background on fairway.

Me today on golf course hill

2016 ON GREEN MOUNTAIN at golf course-UP HILL SPRINTS IN WINTER SNOW-"is good, feels good, gung ho!" in high school. The cold air on my face as the sun set was exhilarating, little icicles hanging from my scarf. I was determined and had a sense of hope. Each hill and long straightaway was a challenge. I loved it.

At Palos Woods Summer 2017

RUNNING TRAINING ATTITUDE and PHILOSOPHY

But let me stop here for a minute and tell you to my philosophy of running. I don't want to talk too much about my life. but I thought you might be interested in my South Side upbringing. I talk more about my running experiences later. Anyway, let's talk about what I learned running all these years in high school and college and give you an idea of my philosophy of training. It probably applies to everybody, but this is really to help that runner who just didn't feel he reached his potential as he got to be nineteen, twenty, twenty-two years old. This is what I did my senior year at Northwestern when I tied a world record of 2:06, two minutes and six seconds, for the 1,000-yard indoor run at the Big Ten Conference Meet. I tied it with Peter Snell of New Zealand, who was one of the outstanding Olympic runners in 1964, I believe it was Tokyo. And he had the world record in both the 800m and 1,500m. You probably heard of him. The race was a come-from-behind victory, which I'll talk about a little later. Remember in 2005 I had dinner with the Highland Park High School track coaches. Peter Snell was

invited and seated next to me. Across from me was Rick Wohlhuter, another former Olympic 800 meter world record holder. What a fantastic thrill it was, 45-50 years ago they set their records (and me too).

But what I learned is how to train smart and take a lot of rest. I guess my mileage, it was twenty to thirty miles a week at Northwestern in college, running indoors. Forty miles a week during cross-country. Outside, it was freezing cold. About 15 to 30 degrees F. Crispy. Bone chilling. But we were inside McGraw Field House, which was cozy. We ran on a dirt track sprinkled with packed down light sand, not the fastest but great for training. We ran around the basketball court, the big stands at one end where we had packed in the shot put and long jump pits, and through a strange aluminum-like metal tunnel that was where the concessions were and underneath the other stands that were built into the building. But it didn't bother me, although it probably detracted from recruiting to some extent compared to the massively beautiful facilities at Wisconsin, Illinois, Michigan State, Michigan, Ohio State and on and on. I know you're interested in the training methods so I'm going to talk about that here and then go on to my story. So please bear with me. This training program assumes you're already in great shape from having run for years and done a lot of cross-country distance running as well. We're talking about starting a new direction for you. This is a two-year program. You have to commit for two years, and you have to really do all of it my way. It's my way or the highway because otherwise it will destroy the rhythm of it. Three different long-distance runners asked me to help them on an informal basis to provide workout ideas. Now they were not part of my program. Each one of them diverted from my advice, felt they had to train even harder and consequently got injured. And one gave up, and the others never reached their potential. You just can't do that because that's running scared. You think if you strain a little harder, you run a little faster you will be better. But it's lack of confidence, that's probably what held these runners back throughout their running career. Although they were good, they didn't reach potential. I did this in New Mexico here, in Albuquerque, and long distance by phone to Chicago from here. All long-distance runners, 5000m.-10000m. They stopped following my advice after a few weeks and injured themselves. Of course, what else would you expect, they didn't follow the program!

READERS NOTES: Why do you need a consistent program?

YOUR WORKOUTS

START 880 HIGH SCHOOL DISTRICT 1965- IN GREEN

So this work out schedule is for to running middle distance, the mile, 800m, 1500m, or anything in between. The premise is that starting in early July and through the summer, you begin preparing by running easy distance. What I recommend is now that you're already in fairly good shape, and you've run for six, eight, ten, twelve years, you don't need to build a gigantic base. But we have to get into shape and get smoothed out and enjoy running. So for the summer, I recommend running, oh, four to seven miles, three or four days a week, starting in late June through the end of August.

By the way, I have these workouts listed in the back of the book. And I just want to give you a taste of it now. When you read the back, you'll see the technical side. But it'll be helpful if you read this entire book to get a feel for running. It's beyond technique. It's beyond workouts. It's who you are, what's inside of yourself that counts. And some people have it, some don't, but it can also be developed. And some of you guys, gals, who have not reached potential haven't really had the gut winning attitude that it takes to reach your highest potential. And so listen to this carefully. I mean every word. I was an

extremely dedicated runner, and I think I ran at my potential and beyond potential, if there is such a thing.

That's all you need to do. You're in shape already. And if you're running four to seven miles, some days you'll jog it easy. Some days, you'll pick it up and fly through it, especially if it's a scenic, interesting place where you like to run. Find scenic, interesting places that bring out your inner motivation and think about being successful, think about winning, think about how this is a long-term program. Imagine yourself winning, not being mediocre, not just doing okay. Think about the flow. I want to discuss flow. It's the flow of your mind and body connected to the earth and the sky. Think of that. You're connected to nature, to Mother Nature. And you're going to flow with the flow of the earth. Of course, the earth before it was polluted and of course in the hubbub of commercialization. A forest preserve with a nice path would be a good place or along a beach, a solid part. We'll go out on the water and soft sand later. Run on grass that grows along a lakeshore, a safe place. Or maybe through your neighborhood. You can design a couple of courses, just be careful of cars. So I want you to enjoy the summer, and I want you to take two weeks off for a vacation in the middle of the summer in July. The warm relaxed days of summer. Don't do any running. Go on a trip to some place you want to see and relax. Okay, runners? Oh, you can also run in a few easy road races or track meets. And a few easy long hill runs. Just have fun.

So as we get into the end of August, now we get to the cross-country season. Some of you will have the opportunity to run in several races. Some of you will be perhaps in a place where it's hard to get to some, but we need to run in a few distance races. 2-3 per month would be ideal. In the Big Ten when I competed, we ran a meet every weekend, starting probably September 20 through early November. I know now runners tend not to run as many meets. But let's try to run four, five or six from September to Thanksgiving (end of November). And these meets don't have to be all championship meets. If you have a championship meet in your area you can get to, go to it. But if you can run the Sunday and Saturday morning 5Ks and 10Ks, as long as you are careful about your knees and your shins. Just run it for fun. See what you can do. You may win these. Try different strategies. Try the strategy where you go out slow back in the pack, and you kick the last 1,200 meters out as hard as you can. Try another strategy where you run the beginning of the race, the first half, push it really hard, the first mile and a half or two on a 5K and see if you can hold on. See what you're made of, tough it out. And other times, run even pace. That's what I want you to do.

But here's the Fall workouts. And there's some variation in this, but this is what I think works and I don't like to change the workouts much. We do pretty much the same workouts week after week. And some of this depends on the terrain and geography and the weather of where you live. As we get near September 1, early in the week, probably Monday, if you're rested enough from a Saturday race, we'll do twenty 400's in the seventies, maybe the sixties if you're really good. But it'll be at a steady cross-country type pace. And a one to two-minute recoup jog in between, depends on the condition you're in. Let's start with two minutes. And I want you to be jogging during the rest. You never stop. You never walk unless you're tight. So if we're on a track, which I prefer not to be, you'll do a recoup jog of maybe 100 to 200 meters. Time every other one or every third 400 and maintain a rhythm. You shouldn't be stressed out. And if you can find a nice level place to run on grass where you won't sprain an ankle, let's do that too. The soccer field at University of New Mexico is fantastic. And if you're on a track, run in flats. But I think we need to get in spikes a lot of the time. They don't have the long training spikes like we used to have so make the best you can do. We used to have a shoe that had a big heel but made with spikes in the front. I don't know. Try to see if you can find one of those made of kangaroo hide. Maybe do 12 400's in flats and 8 in spikes.

So we will go with twenty (20) 400's on Monday. Now Tuesday, I want an easy run to recuperate. It's up to you, four to seven miles. Don't always push for seven. And you can start out easy and kind of pick the pace up to just cross-country pace in the middle or end. You might be starting out well into the 6's and finish up in the 5's somewhere. Some of you might run that last mile around close to five. But let's not really push it too hard. Wednesday, we come back to another interval workout of some type, and I would recommend four one-mile intervals or three times a mile and a half [4 x 1 mile or 3 x 1.5 miles]. Make sure you always jog a mile warm-up and a mile warm-down. And if we're doing these longer interval miles and up, don't do it on a track. Find a nice level course on a softer surface, like grass or soft earth, dirt. And, you know, we can start these -- these would be run in the mid-5s, I'm thinking for a 4:10 miler or a 1:51 or 1:52 half-miler. And then we work down as you get better towards five. And some of you will be running these in the high 4's, 4:50, 4:45. We might run a few in the 5:00, 5:30 range and try to break 5:00 on the last one. It should be a fairly hard workout but always maintain rhythm. If you aren't maintaining rhythm slow down. And if you're really dead, just quit the workout. It's hard to do. It takes brains to do that. We've got to train smart, not just hard. And things have to be in rhythm and balance.

Thursday, again, would be a four- to seven-mile paced cross-country run. On this one it depends. We'll start easy but try to do two or three miles close to, at least cross-country effort. Okay? But let's not kill ourselves. I want one day of no running or a very easy warm up. And I think that's Friday. You need a day off. Just don't run, period, or only loosen up, a very easy 2 mile jog. Saturday would be a race or a fairly hard workout. We could have a two- to three-mile time trial. We could also go with thirty to forty-five minutes of intense fartlek (a Swedish word that laterally means "to wander around aimlessly"), translated as Speed Play. It combines aerobic and anaerobic training. I call it free form interval running. There are different ways to do this. I've seen it where you run, jog for a minute, run hard for two minutes, jog for a minute, run hard for 3 minutes and on and on. Or find a park, golf course, forest, or woods as I would -- or down a course even in a city street, or alternate. Jog for a half mile, to warm up, stride for a quarter mile or a half mile, then a sprint, but an easy sprint for a hundred or two hundred meters. Keep mixing it up. Keep rest intervals brief. Run towards a landmark like a tree or hill. But you have got to push it so at the end you're really, really tired, and you're just pushing beyond your strength close to your maximum, but maybe not quite if you are overstraining.

And Sunday, an easy run. We don't have to run ten miles. We can run three or four miles. The first couple, you might be stiff. Just loosen up and maybe somewhere in the last mile, you sort of pick it up again at that cross-country pace and bring it in. And that's it. And I don't believe in double workouts. Never did them. Except I did them my freshman year thanks to my friend, Peter Davis, who was my fraternity brother on the NU Cross-Country Team and friend from senior year at high school. In fact, he got me to go to Northwestern. He was a good cross-country runner. He used to pull me out of bed in the dorm freshmen year, and we'd run three miles, four miles hard at 7:00 in the morning. And I'd be chasing right after him. He was one of the outstanding runners on Northwestern's cross-country team that won the title that year in 1965 at the Big Ten Conference Meet and second in the NCAA. Those teammates are Craig Boydston, Lee Assenheimer, John Duffield, Pat Edmondson, Peter Davis, and Steve Cullinan. Congratulations to you guys. I trained with them. It wasn't easy.

So this is how I want you to just repeat this. Week after week, basically, the same workouts, the same pattern. We don't mix it up. There's no reason to mix it up. And it'll develop a rhythm. And you'll see yourself improve. If somewhere mid-season, you're tiring out, take a week off or take four days off, Thursday to Sunday. You're not going to lose conditioning. You can't improve when you're running too

tired. It's just a struggle. You won't like it. And it doesn't do your muscles and cardiovascular system any good to train when you're really beat from other workouts. Your muscles are torn down, and your blood sugar level is low. And you just don't have it. I'd like to see you train with some zest, and that's why we only train hard three days a week. Now if you look at the miles in this, what are we talking? Maybe forty tops. If you count the rest intervals and the warm-ups and warm-downs, thirty-five to forty is enough for all of you now restarting or recharging your career with...a new zest and flow.

We run this cross-country season through the Fall, into December. Now it also depends what your climate is. If it's winter, we start to switch over to indoor track workouts somewhere in December. And I would recommend in December, you take a week off. Don't run. Let your legs recoup. If you need ten days, take ten days. You're not going to lose training. And remember, the major goal in this is not to get injured, not to get sick, not to get stale. Running tears you down. And if you over do it, you will get injured. Then you're also more likely to get sick because your immune system goes down and you get tired and worn out. So I want to keep you guys and gals fresh as a daisy, as they say here in America. Okay, folks? So let's keep with the program. So from July to December we build a base of endurance running (5 months). "No base, then no good race!!!" [My Comment]

The indoor workouts (or outdoors if in a warm climate) would be as follows. You transition into this from mid-November, after cross-country season, to late December. During this period, I ran 20 x 220-yard intervals weekly (sometimes twice) with a 90 second rest (eventually 45 seconds). But let your body guide you. In early January the college indoor season would begin. Now the structured weekly workouts began in earnest. On *Mondays* we would go with eight to ten interval 400s. It depends on your conditioning. These would be in the low-mid 60s. Maybe we'll start mid- to upper-60s. But if you're going for a sub-4:10 mile or a sub-1:50 half-mile I'd say low to mid-60s. But you have got to be smooth. You'll work these times down over the season. This is going to be a workout you're going to run most of the season on *Mondays.* (Substitute the 20 x 200's every second or third week). The rest interval would start with the 200-meter jog, a couple of minutes or so. And we'll get it down to less than that eventually. And when you run ten of these 400's that's two and a half miles, with your jog it's another mile plus, that's three and a half, and then the warm up and warm down, and a little striding. You get in a five-mile workout. I really don't like the idea of you running in flats, nor do I like racing shoes. Get the sturdiest spikes you can find. Somewhere on the Internet, eBay. You've got to have these old-fashioned spikes that have built up heels, (as I have already said). That's what we need to train in. And if you just run in flats, when we do the intervals, you won't develop the right muscles and the right form. So the worst case scenario just get a sturdy, sturdy pair of track shoes if you can't find the style with the elevated heels and spikes. Heart and Sole Shoes here in Albuquerque has distance race shoes with a built-up heel and front spikes.

Tuesday, is going to be a slow day, a rest day. What I did, I would run three miles indoors in full sweats. I like you running in sweats. I want you to sweat a lot, legs, pants and a sweatshirt. And if you're in a super hot climate, we probably can do without it, I don't want you to fall over! But I also want you to really warm up. And we'll do, what I call, slow-medium-fast miles consecutively. In other words, a three-mile run in which the first mile might be closer to seven minutes, the second mile around six, and the third around five. You run consecutively indoors. You run in the outside lane. It should be smooth. And it will do two things: one is you loosen yourself up from yesterday's harder workout to prepare for the next day. And two it gets you some endurance. You'd be surprised. By the time you get to that third mile, you're pushing 5:00, 5:15, 4:45 in flats only. One of my training guys, a college distance star, had a hard time doing it. You run in flats. And that's all you do. We don't run sprints. We don't do straightaways. We don't try to go out and bust a five or ten-mile run because it will drain you and I'll drop you if I am your coach. I have zero tolerance for runners who don't follow the plan because what's the point. It'll defeat the plan. And I don't want a bunch of defeated runners on my hands, and I don't want you to feel defeated.

Wednesday, we're back to intervals. And there's variety here. So I'm going to give you several different workouts. One is 4 x 800m. We recoup jog four to six hundred meters in between. This is going to give you some distance. Now I ran these around the equivalent of about a 2:03 or 2:04 800m, but I was in shape to run a sub-1:50 half-mile. So, you know, we'll see, 2:05, 2:10, 2:12. You can run the first three easier and pick up the last one. They should be smooth. Everything we run is smooth with rhythm with a little pick-up on these.

Another workout, and this is even for a half-miler, is a mile and a half fast [2400 meters]. My best was 6:42. That's pretty good. So you jog your mile, do some easy straightaways. This is a time trial. And then do another mile or so of easy jogging afterwards. And when you warm up and warm down, I want the

sweat pants on and the sweatshirt, even if you're indoors. And the only way you don't wear them if the temperature is over 85 outside, over 90. Okay? Even then, you might put the sweat pants on just to make sure your legs are nice and sweaty and supple.

Another workout is two times three-quarters or 1200 meters. Again, you know, I used to run these around 3:04, 3:07. You could run these at that pace. You could run them in the teens, 3:10, 3:15 or slower at 3:20, and pick up the next one. And your rest interval is an easy 5 minute 800 meter jog. Okay? That's all you do. Could you run three of them? Not now. Maybe later in the season. But we're not training for cross-country. That's what we do there. When I was a 21-year-old Senior, I ran a 2:55 in practice outdoors by myself in the middle of a workout. It felt good. Try one yourself. That's fast!!

For a little variety, we could go 200, 400, 600, 800, 600, 400 and 200, but again at a moderate pace, 30 on the 200, 62-64 on the 400, 1:38-42 on the 600, 2:04-2:10 on the 800 and down with a 200 or 400 jog in between. It's your choice. This workout is slower with less rest intervals but you can always stride in the last one for some speed if you feel good →27 to 28 for the last 200.

***Thursday r*epeat Tuesday, it's the three-mile run again, seven, six, five minutes. *Friday,* we take an easy jog, just a race warm-up. *Saturday,* we have a race or a time trial. Now I raced from early January through the end of March continuously, a race every weekend. A lot of times, I ran three races. I'd run the mile, the 880 and the anchor of the mile relay (4 X 400m). Back then we called it the mile relay. So I know it will be hard for you guys, if you're not in college, to race this often and to run three races. But see what you can do. And you can run local races. If you search the paper in a big city, there's going to be some. You can get in as an open runner. And if you're good enough, you might get invited to a few big Invitationals. The Mt. SAC Relays in California is a good one if you live out west. Last year 6th in the 800m was 1:47.29, or a 1:48 for an 880, which is about what I ran when in top shape in 1969. 12th was 1:49.66. This is for elite runners. Some of you can be competitive here. Of course Clayton Murphy set a world best time of 1:43.66 this year in 2018. For the 1500m 3:50 is a good time, which is a 4:08 mile. Many of you can enter this race and be competitive. The Elite final went in 3:42 or about 3:59. We will rest a lot for these.**

Sunday **is a three-mile easy run. Start slow, you'll probably be stiff. And again, as you get to the last 800 meters or 1,200 meters try to pick it up a little, push it some, as long as you aren't going to feel tight and strain a muscle. Again, we don't want to get injured.**

One of the interesting things about getting into great shape is even when you train you run times you never thought possible. Power and confidence just coming oozing out of your skin as you fly around the practice track. I once ran a 1:50 indoors in practice by myself when I was peaking. It was easy too. Otherwise you just tend to struggle and never reach the "Power Zone".

So every-other week (on *Monday*) we're going to alternate. If we ran 400s last Monday, this week we're going to run twenty times 200 slow, 29 - 32, depends on your ability. And we want to get down to the point where our rest interval is maybe forty-five seconds. And we can just jog in a semi-circle and walk a little of this. We don't want to jog a full 200. And what we'll do is slowly work it down. So if you're running 29 to 30 when you're in top shape with a forty-five second rest interval, that's about what I did. And then maybe the last one, you're feeling smooth, you run a 27. That's your speed work. Running fast and SMOOTH when you are tired.

Let's talk about speed work. There's no real speed work in my training, just a little outdoors, or on the relay, because, remember, what is a 1:48 800 meter race? It's a four times twenty-seven seconds interval workout with a zero interval rest. A four-minute mile is four times sixty seconds with a zero interval rest. It's an amusing thing to keep in mind, but we don't need to be running that fast. Now I did run those 440-yard races as the anchor in the relay, and I'm not sure how. I would like to squeeze a few of those in. So if we have an off week, we can run a time trial, an 800 or 1200. Then we'll take a 15-minute walk, or jog, and then run a hard 400 at 49-52 on our own or with a buddy, a pacer. So we'll get in that kind of speed work. We're not going to run repetitive speed work outs in practice. That's the key to this. It's rhythm, building pace and endurance. Okay? I want to be clear on this. So we're going to repeat this for eight, ten, twelve weeks. Now if we get a really super big meet, we're going to modify it. What we'll do is, after we run our Sunday loosening up run, on Monday, we'll run six or eight times 200 slow, even if you're a half-miler. We're just going to loosen up around 30-33. *Tuesday* for the half-milers, we'll run three 400s with an easy 400 jog in the mid-50s around pace, 55, 53, 57, as long as it's smooth. A 1:54 800m runner would run a little bit slower. For the milers, we're going to run four times 400, and we're going to run it around pace, which will be around 60-65. If a sub-4:06 miler we could run a 62, a

60, a 57, and maybe a 64, if we're feeling up for it. And our rest intervals shouldn't be too short. We want to get a good two-minute rest interval but always jogging. Okay? Also 400-800-400 works well at 62; 1:58-2:02; 64

***Wednesday*, we'll run the seven, six, five, three-mile paced workout, which is guaranteed to loosen you up. *Thursday,* do an easy race warm-up, that's about a mile of easy jogging and some really easy strides. The race is on Saturday, or Sunday. *Friday,* take another easy, pre-race jog warm-up. *Saturday*, you race most likely. You should be fresh for this and tuned. And you got to have the right attitude. We're going to run with balance. We're not going to run afraid. If we're a frontrunner, we're going to take the lead. And if it's one of these races I see on television where everybody crawls, you're not going to crawl with them. You're going to run your pace, even if you're out in front because, to me, the crawl, that's the chicken way to run. I've seen seventy-second first laps in the national meet in Oregon. It was terrible. It's no way to race. And we don't want to have it all down to a sprint at the end because I'm sure a lot of you aren't great sprinters. At the Rio de Janeiro Brazil 2016 Olympics the 1500m final was won in a SLOW 3:50! The winner ran a 51 second last 400m. He trained for it by running 5x400 in 50-52 about 3 weeks before the race. Maybe number 2,3,4, or 5 would have won the race if the pace was at their best effort and a world class result of 3:30-3:35. He was ready for a super-fast finish. But somebody always is a good sprinter and can have a fluke race win, even if they aren't the best runner. So, we want to push these. Then we're going to move to outdoor season-where the challenge is to not get stale. More on outdoor season later.**

This weekend at the NCAA 800m the top 8 runners finished within about one second of one another, and all ran the final 400m in 53-54 seconds. The pace was slow and the 1500m winning time of 3:43 was slow, (a 4:00 mile pace). Third place went to a New Mexico runner in 3:43.5. He ran a 3:37 in the semi-final and had a best 1500m time of 3:35. If he had pushed the pace, he might have won at a quicker time. It was a desperate sprint to the finish race for everyone, a bad strategy.

SOME ECONOMIC CHARTS AND A DRIVE THROUGH MY HOMETOWN

And now we take a break and move on to a quick discussion of economics and then back to track.

THE SURGE (the economic one from 1945-1975)

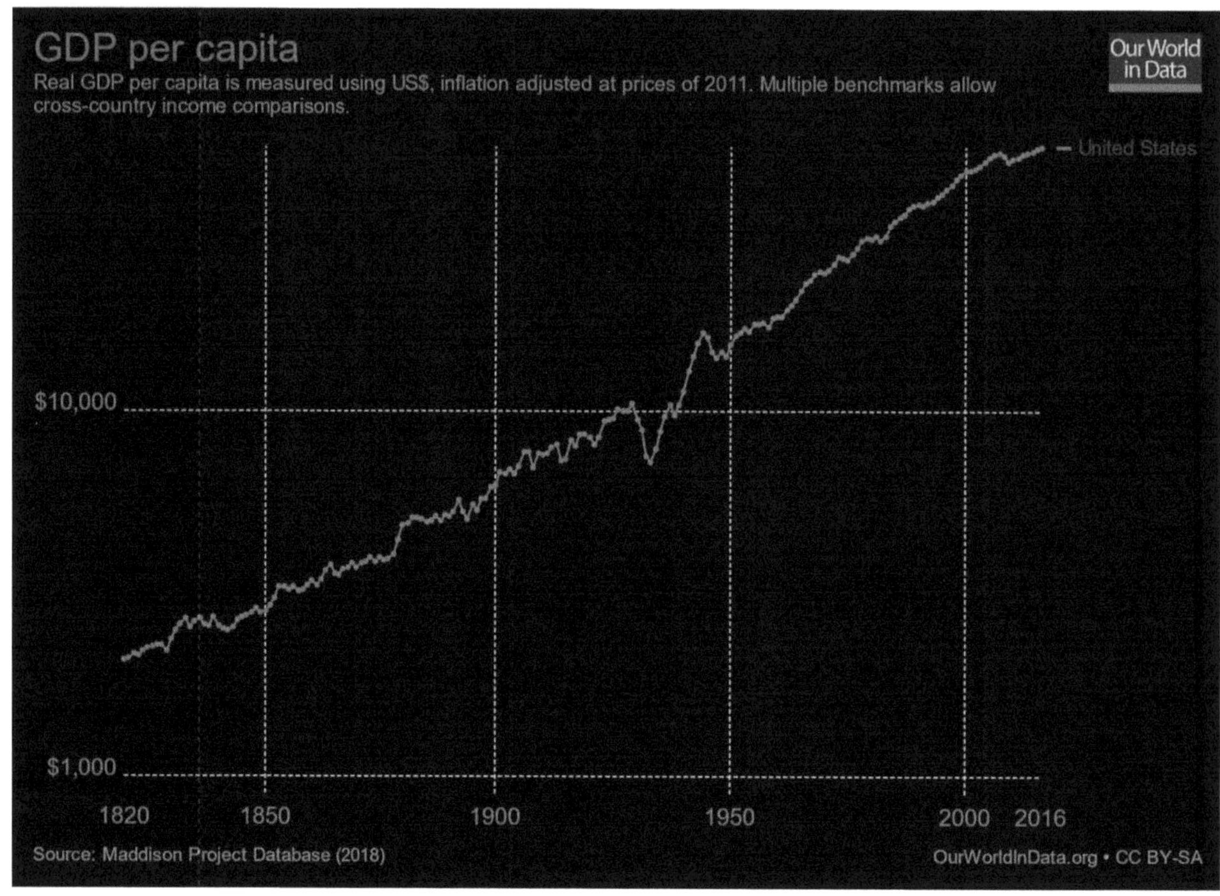

THE MIRACLE US GDP PER CAPITA 200 YEARS

You see I told you this book is titled "other stuff" so here is some. Some of my personal ideas and beliefs and observations about America. So athletes can't have thoughts about anything but sports?? Hey, I'm 70 years, so here goes. What I have learned (I think).

So now we are going to change directions and talk about the ***SURGE,*** the economic and societal environment, after WW II. Then I'll finish with some of the highlights of my career from age 14-24 and a few other observations. Remember today I am an economics instructor at *Central New Mexico Community College* and was a history major at Northwestern University, had an A average in history. A great school and history department. Robert Wiebe was an American history professor who really inspired me. Believe it or not I wrote a paper under his guidance called "The Economic Aspects of Social Change" And I still have that interest today. 50 years later. I'm always looking hard at world events, news, and am a truth seeker. I am also very interested in Russia. I put the concept of the SURGE in this book because it reflects the feeling of growing up in the 1950's and 1960's, which influenced athletic ideals and performance. We looked outward with optimism and ran for honor and glory-no lucrative stipends, endorsements, and training camps in those days. We were lucky we got a few pairs of shoes. I had to ask the Puma rep for a pair. And no performance drugs either. Great track and field athletes today can become very comfortable financially with some incomes over $100,000 to $1 million dollars plus. It's "Show Me the Money! "But I can't think of one reason the shoe companies should make huge profits and not share it with more athletes. In fact, the second tier athletes, those ranked 4th-20th should ALSO GET FREE TRAINING, room, board, a moderate stipend and a part-time job. The Cult of the Celebrity Athlete, Movie Star, permeates American society now. Those at the top make enormous sums, while the rest of us struggle along or earn more reasonable incomes. Unfortunately, that's the currently popular idea.

We need to balance that out for America to achieve steady economic growth and opportunity for all as in the 1945-75 years. We need more inclusive training camps. Hello NIKE? NEW BALANCE? ADIDAS? And other major companies and wealthy people? And let's try a little more cooperation and less cutthroat competition in society. It would be better for everyone. Right now I am thinking about the University of Chicago Track Club run by the venerable Ted Haydon from 1960-1985. The Club, a real democracy, and a kind place, open minded, accepting.

IN EVERGREEN PARK TODAY

Anyway, today, August 2016, my friend Merrilyn and I are driving in Evergreen Park (our former home town where we graduated from high school) at 92nd and Troy, heading towards where the Aqua Park (community swimming complex) was or still is. I used to walk this street. I used to walk home from Aqua

Park all summer as well. That was a two-mile walk each way, or I'd ride my bicycle. So I was always biking or walking all summer. Occasionally I had to run home when in high school, about a mile, to make my 10 PM curfew. Ran like the wind, sweating like a steam engine. Did this constantly - so it's interesting. That's part of this whole phenomena of moving, being full of exercise. And not always driving around in a car. Evergreen Park is a suburb adjacent to the Southwest corner of Chicago.

We stopped by the Evergreen Park High School track where I used to run and the area around the high school. The prairie and open space were behind my home where there were trails we used to run on and play explorer and do adventuresome things. Look, here's a park I used to play baseball in too. I used to walk a mile or two each way or ride my bike to middle school, 7-8th grade, age 13-14. And no rides from any parents in those days. Uh-uh, no way. I was more fortunate in High School –had about a long 2 block walk over some Grand Trunk Railroad tracks. The Grand Trunk is long gone. America's 15 or so railroads in 1960 are now combined into only four mega railroads. It's not as interesting as when each railroad represented a unique characteristic of its region and had their own logo and colors. When I was 12 we used to leave pennies on the rails and watch those freight trains roar by and flatten the coins. Speaking of trains, I have just gotten a 1970 Lionel model electric train, can't wait to put it up and just watch it run, round and round. That's what old guys do. Hah!

But anyway, there it is. The pool, the parks, the track, the schools, all these places where I grew up. It hasn't changed at all except the trees are bigger, forty, fifty years of growth. A few new houses, but not real new ones. They all look the same as in 1965. Yeah, I see it, I feel it. The pool. It hasn't changed. Three big pools, different sizes: big, medium and small for kids. Huge diving boards. Look at them. Slides. And it was all we did. There was nothing private. I mean, it was a public place for the community. I can still smell the chlorine. Yeah. Well, the pool has no water in it. And it has weeds growing all over. It's not being utilized. They used to sell inexpensive family memberships to it. But in any event, there it is. It's a ghost town. Part of the conditioning was getting a suntan over the summer and the long long trek to the pool.

So the town, the community of Evergreen Park, where I grew up, I see it as a continuing surge of labor, work, striving. It was and still seems to be a surge that represents industrial ingenuity and opportunity, success, stability. *IT'S THE MODERATE MIDDLE CLASS THAT AROSE AFTER WW II.* It's progressed from generation to generation. It's the momentum, the engine, the power of the country really. This type of community, many just like it, really built the United States. It's the secret weapon or the secret formula, I would say, of this country. All the similar communities, towns, cities in the USA. I not only see it, I feel it. It may not be exciting, but it's reliable. So maybe it's not as much as impressive as the powerful military and national security state that gives us international influence and respect, but the people at home, going about their lives, building, succeeding, having a sense of freedom to grow and develop- that's the REAL POWER in my opinion.

Buckingham Fountain Chicago

So all these stores and parks and people. And now it is my generation, us baby boomers, born in 1945-1963, that are running things. So here in Evergreen Park, Illinois, and similar towns are everyday people, some still here since 1946. Or their kids. And I don't mean that derogatorily either. Just responsibly then and now going about their business of life and learning and working. This is like a great stabilization power. It's the power that builds GDP, real economic growth of three or four or five percent a year, and not zero, one or two, speaking as an economist. No malaise then. And that sequence, that expectation that you would do better or well, and doors would be opened for making a good living and a good lifestyle, earning adequate money or more than enough ...trying a to lead a responsible life--that was all available. It was. It's eroding now, at least that's what the experts tell us. And it becomes apparent in some places that the erosion is taking out some of the momentum and power very slowly. It's like a river losing its momentum over time, you hardly see it. But it slows down, gets less powerful. It drains off here and there. There's less water flowing into it from upstream. That's sort of what I envision this country as kind of going through. But the surge, that strength, you can still -- you can feel it here still. It exists in this area that we're driving through, Evergreen Park, Oaklawn, suburbs like it, Palos Hills, Chicago Heights. Yeah, it's more multi-cultural than it was, which is good because the country is too and things have changed. And let's not forget about cities like Milwaukee, Cleveland, Pittsburgh, Detroit, and Buffalo, full of hard-working immigrants and their children. I traveled to Detroit many times when it had a bustling downtown with tall buildings and and a buzz of business. It seemed to be like an Eastern city. I think the automobile companies gave it an international orientation and also a connection to Washington DC where executives went on important business. I liked it.

We see it here. The owners passed the house on. They transferred ownership. The new generations are here now. I see them here outside on the front porch or watering the lawn. the new and older generations, with still a possibility of a new economic surge. I think that it's the day-to-day momentum and the economic power that just builds, and it's kind of taken for granted that it moves people along the track of progress, whether it's socially together interacting or working together. It's this whole lifestyle. Today, too much of that gets diverted into much fewer upper income economic hands. Celebrity richness, opulence, people being told how great it is to be rich. But the dream then was, you see, not to dream about being there, or to become one of them. It's not the dream of moving from Evergreen Park say to a town like Winnetka, a very nice wealthy suburb (or Greenwich, Mclean, Shawnee Mission, Scottsdale, Gross Pointe, Shaker Heights). Though that may appeal to certain people. But to most people then, the dream was just the good feeling of being within this surge of a positive life and not always looking out, wishing you had something else, but having what you want and developing yourself just a little bit more in your own life and with your relatives and children and so on, and grandchildren. So it's an organic process of being part of something you already have and not looking from the outside in, wishing you were elsewhere, SEARCHING for the American Dream, BECAUSE YOU ALREADY were in IT. The surge pulled and tossed us baby boomers out into the world full of hope and expectations that the USA would take care of us, give us a chance to show what we could do, live, give us a footing, a direction. Now I'm not so sure. It doesn't seem as clear.

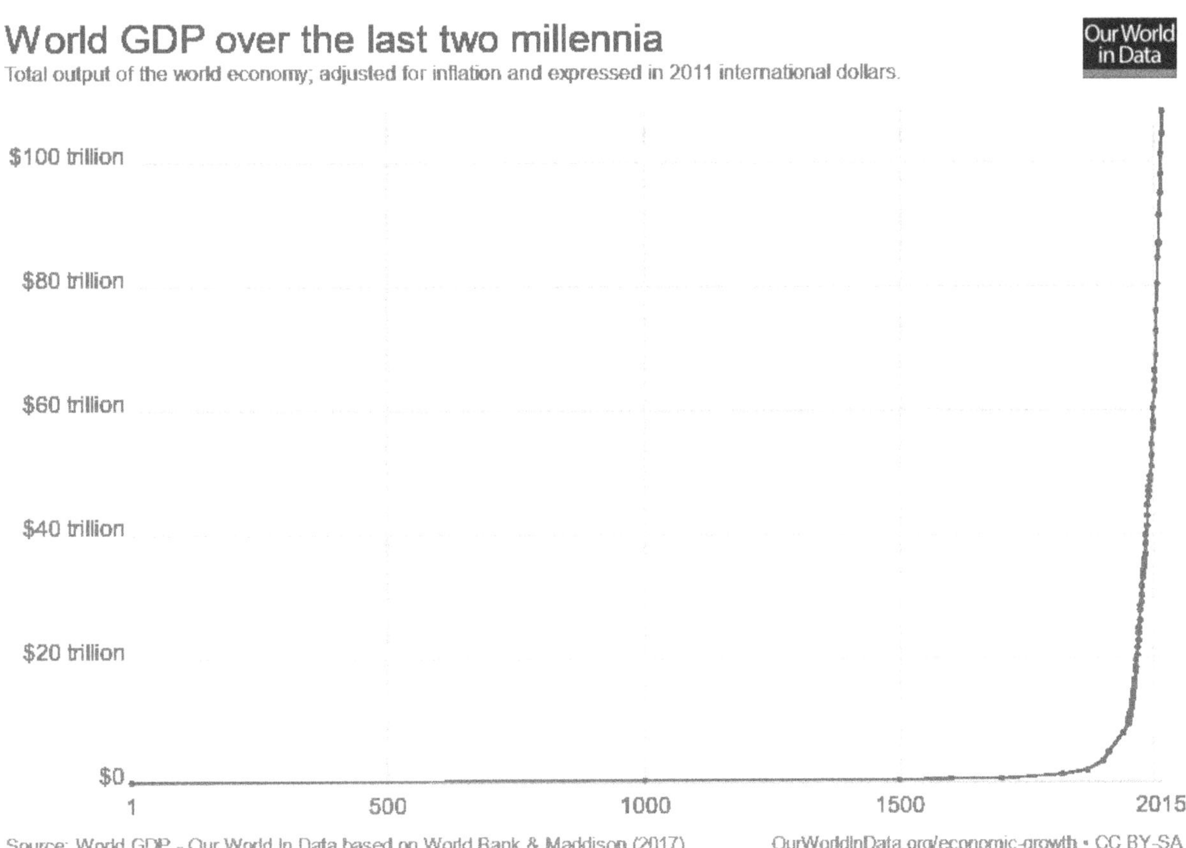

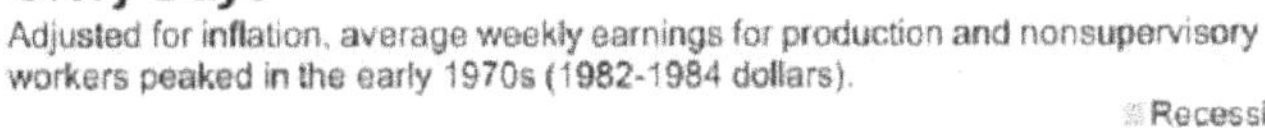

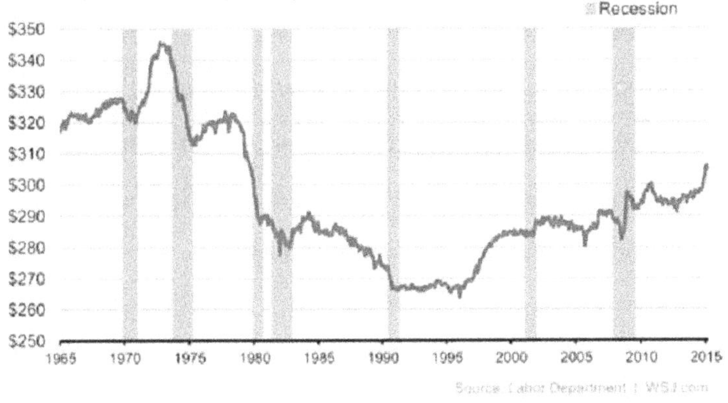

MEDIAN WAGE GROWTH USA 1970 -2015 DECLINE ADJUSTED FOR INFLATION FOR PRODUTION AND NON-SUPERVISORY WORKERS

Median Household income net of inflation unchanged since 1999.

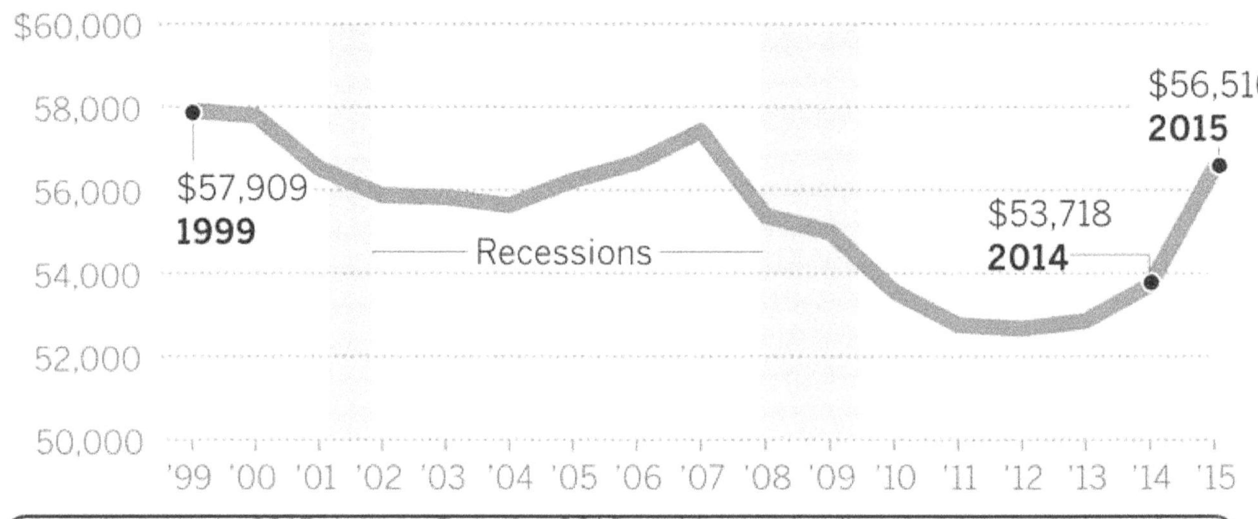

I'm nervous about flying, and it comes and goes, the nervousness. As I get older, I don't fly as much, and I get more nervous. It's the insecurity of not knowing how it will go. I guess the flight, is kind of similar to living your life now and being increasingly aware of its insecurities and wondering how you will make it. But anyway, the whole world is going places today and tomorrow, across the ground at high altitudes and super-fast speeds. The USA doesn't seem so much a surge sometimes as a chaotic and random turbulence- gets you there all right, but the ride is no fun anymore for a lot of people.

MORE ABOUT TRACK:

Now back to track and running. One of the things I want to emphasize is your thinking and feelings before races. I have to say before key races I was really very nervous and frightened, I guess, maybe more than some. But it helped me to run good performances and emphasize the importance of what I was going to do. I guess because I grew up feeling that I had to survive I had to win. To me, racing, the big races was really, and I'll be honest with you, there was no in between. It was either winning or having a successful race time or both. And you didn't just lose. Losing was something you had to accept, but, at the same time, before the race, it was a very strong feeling of urgency and fear. That adrenaline really got me going. I said that in the banquet at Northwestern University in January of 2011 when I was inducted into the Athletic Hall of Fame in front of a dinner crowd of about 200 people, that winning, and racing was a matter of life or death to me. It was not just a pastime. It was the integral part of my life. And I did get huge highs from winning and getting all the fame and glory and newspaper articles and pictures. I have huge scrapbooks. There was so much. I suppose it was unhealthy, but I lived for it. It was an addiction and a narcotic of emotion. But I'm just telling you how I was. I probably still am to some extent, although I've mellowed out. The nice thing about that banquet were the people I invited who were at my table. There was of course my proud son Blaine, a former terrific 400m runner, Dr. Steve Cullinan, a former teammate and his fiance Patty, Rich Nayer, coach of the newly formed Chicago Track Club and a friend, and Zeus and Toni Preckwinkle. Zeus ran for UCTC and was my friend and a big supporter of me and still is now. He now lives in the Philippines. Toni was the only woman member of the City of Chicago City Council for years. What a battle-she was their conscience. She got scattered site public housing into Chicago to replace those horrible 12 story apartment buildings built years ago that became full of gang violence and were austere, crowded, in poor condition. They did not uplift people. Now she is President of Cook County (Chicago metro area), a very important position, on a level with the Illinois Governor, and the Mayor of Chicago, Rahm Emanuel (also a Northwestern graduate). Zeus and Tony are graduates of The University of Chicago, like me. I felt very honored to have all of them there. Jim Noe, Chuck Porter and Gerald Smith were also there, all NU great runners. Gerald held the school record in the 400m run. Chuck and Jim are members of the Riis Park Striders in Chicago, a great track club.

The week before that Big Ten record in 1969, I remember on a Tuesday I was studying. Of course, the big race was Saturday and the preliminary on Friday. And all of a sudden, the jitters hit me right in my stomach, you know, the butterflies. And they wouldn't go away. I had to function all week going to school, sleeping, eating, conversing, doing some light training with those butterflies. They just stuck with me. And before I ran that race I was just, I guess I was terrified of losing. I had put so much on the line for eight years and my two biggest rivals ran the same race, the 1,000-yard run. Why one of them could have chosen the 880 instead is beyond me. But there the three of us were at the starting line, standing and staring at each other. And I got up to the line just dreading this. My legs felt like concrete. I was really worried, but I flew. I won. I beat my rivals. But back to that race later.

Leading Big 10 preliminary heat 1969

OUTDOORS – END OF SEASON WORKOUTS.

So outdoor season is tricky in America. Now if you're maybe in Asia or in Africa, or also parts of Europe, you don't have a switch of indoor and outdoor seasons. The end of cross-country season might be March if you're in Kenya and your competitive racing season sort of starts going in the spring and it extends all through the summer into September. So you have to move my workouts around the calendar. But we'll say outdoor season for the US starts in April, and that would be the preliminary outdoor season for you runners in other continents if you don't have an indoor racing season. So take that as an understanding. You still would have to run the indoor season workouts as a base. Okay? Whatever time of the year that was, maybe the January workouts will start in April and run to June. Then these workouts are really the racing season workouts later in the summer. They probably look easy. But lookout for staleness!

April was cold and windy and rainy in the upper-Midwest US. Some of the days were beautiful. Others, we had tornados or just really cold 44 degree weather. I didn't run well in cold weather. But we trained through it. And again, the end of March, early April, I kind of did two or three weeks of interval endurance training again to reset myself so to speak, like rebooting the computer after a strenuous, hard indoor racing season.

So I would just take this two-week endurance stint perhaps early in April. I'd go back to running interval 440s, perhaps on a Monday. I might run twenty 440's just like cross-country season, slow. Tuesday a three to five mile run at an increasing pace in a nice interesting place. If you feel inspired just let it out. Wednesday, three 1200s, slow. Slow for me was 3:15, 3:25, (for a 4:05- 4:10 miler.) Thursday a quick 2 to 3-mile warm-up. Friday, a 1 to 2-mile warm-up, see a movie and have a juicy cheeseburger!

And then we'd race on Saturday or do a fairly hard 45 minute fartlek. And it could be cold outside, you know. Those first few races, I might run a slow 4:20 mile, 1:56 880 and a 50 second 440 relay split because the weather was cold, windy, although sometimes by the second or third week of the season, we'd get a nice sixty- to seventy-degree day to pop up. That's usually when I started running well. I remember Sophomore year, 1967. We flew up to the University of Minnesota the second week of April, a beautiful day. It had been two years since my 1:52 High School 880. I just hadn't let out a real good race and was getting discouraged. But! The extra endurance training paid off and I ran a 4:14 mile (2nd), a 1:52 880 (1st) and a 49 relay split. I was back!! There is a difference between being in shape and REALLY being in shape. I knew I had finally reached that higher level. But as far as workouts are concerned, the first weeks I'd emphasize some endurance interval training. And then by the third week, we'd come down to something like this. Assuming we had run a race on Saturday, Sunday again would be the three-mile easy run where once we're loosened up, the last mile or 800, I'd pick it up, kind of like pushing it a little, a little faster than cross-country pace. Monday, we had some variation here. We'd do six to eight 440s. And again, around sixty, sixty-three AND A LAST ONE IN 56-58 SECONDS SMOOTH. Remember, always smooth, no grimacing, straining. Tuesday is the recovery (7-6-5 minute pace) 3 mile run again. Wednesday a mildly hard workout. Maybe 8-10 x 200 in 28-29 with a smooth 26-27 on the last one. That's your speed workout portion. We could also put these 200's on Monday instead of the 400's. Another might be a ladder, 200-400-800-400-200 slower than race pace. 30-62-2.04-62-28 with a 2-minute jog rest interval. This is for a 1:50 half miler or a 4:10 miler. Or instead a solid 1200m at race pace (3:00-3:10), then some easy striding. A 4:20 miler would run 3:15, a 4:30 miler a 3:21. BE CAREFUL, you can run too hard and that's it for the weekend race. You'll tighten up then, because you ran your race in practice. Many runners do this, but it doesn't count. NO practice awards. Thursday and Friday we loosen up easily and probably race on Saturday (or a time trial). All run FRESH. Sounds too easy? It might be. But I learned a lesson. Most of the bad races I ran occurred with a great very hard workout on Tuesday. ---(Actual Result / Capability --) NAAU 1969 [1:51/1:47]; Olympic Tryouts 1968 [1:51/1:48] Drake Relays 1969 [4:11/4:04]. Get the picture?

You can also really get stale at the end of the outdoor season if you start pushing hard speed interval workouts and practice time-trials. This is when the BIG Races are starting, and you need to be fresh. So error on the side of doing too little. You already are in great shape! I believe most of the intensive anaerobic fast interval workouts did not help me, like 6 x 330 hard; or 4 x 220 almost all out, or an all out 600. So now at BIG RACE TIME in May and June we switch our routine to Monday, 6-8 x 150 strides to loosen up. Tuesday 3 x 400 smooth 53-57 (800m race); or 4 x 400 @ 58-63 (mile race); or 200-400-800-400-200; at 60-65 pace. We could also run a 1200m at 90% (3:03-for a 4:04 mile or 3:08 for a 4:10 miler), but no hard kick. That's it. Wednesday 7-6-5 three mile run. Thursday and Friday some easy warming up. Saturday-the BIG ONE. As fresh as a daisy, legs bouncy, ready to go. This is when it counts, what you have trained for the past year. Just begin the race and let your training and instincts take over. Try not to worry too much, be happy. You can do it. Put yourself on the line-now or never-no excuses.

You could also take a smooth easy cross-country run on an off week too, maybe 4 miles starting easy and picking up the pace. A build-up, fine tuning your body, with a low stress factor. You could also do a blast workout the prior week or two before an upcoming BIG race. If the race is on the 21stth then run this between the 10th to the 14th--2 X 400 FAST (48-53) with a full rest interval jog (5 minutes?) or 2 x 800 in 1:52-1:58--, with the slow one first. Full rest jog like the 400's. Or an all-out 1200m (2:55-3:02). Then a long easy warm-down, to get the lactic acid out of your system. (These practice times are for sub 1:52 800m and sub 4:12 mile runners.)

As an aside, just to let you know, Lee Evans, the Olympic great world record 400-meter runner in 1968, would run 3 x 300 meters in 33 seconds in practice with a 7 minute rest. But he was a sprinter.

I made the big mistake of running 2 x 400 in 48-49 hard on a Tuesday practice before the Olympic tryout Saturday in 1968. I felt great in practice at 7300-foot elevation. I should have run 52-53 coasting instead. Well I faded in the race, just didn't have it. I was last in 1:52. But my Big 10 rivals, Ron Kuchinski of Michigan and Mark Winzenreid of Wisconsin, finished #3 and #4. Ron made the Olympic team. I could have been in that 1:48 pack, might have made the team as #3. BUT I ran my race in practice on Wednesday. That didn't count. I beat both of them 5 months later at the Big 10 Meet when I tied the World Record. I also had won the 880 my Sophomore year at IOWA just ahead of Ron. They were fantastic runners. I am still in touch with Mark on Facebook.

I also have to tell all of you that during that summer I went on a Study trip to Russia (Soviet Union) to learn the language and culture with the Northwestern University Russian language department rather than going directly to the all summer long Olympic Training Camp at South Lake Tahoe, California. There I continued to train very hard, but mostly endurance type running and fast intensive fartlek. I never touched a track. I ran in parks, streets, and sand hills and beaches (near Finland). No races, no intervals. But it worked. I came back in shape ready to go. At the Olympic Camp at the end of August I did track training to tune up for the tryout. But I crammed in too much in a brief time. But I still ran those fast 400's, and I didn't need any speed training. I think this proves a point. Ask Peter Snell of New Zealand. He did pretty much the same thing over the course of a season. He wrote that he believed he could have run an all-out 400m with one breath. If I only had not run those 400's sooooo fast. Maybe 51-53, that would have been enough, optimal.

I made that mistake again at the NAAU Meet (National USA Championship) in Miami Florida in 1969. Mark Winzenreid and I ran a great workout on Tuesday before that BIG MEET. We ran 20 x 200 in the humid Miami heat at 29-30 seconds and smoothly blasted the last 200 in about 22 + seconds. My fastest 200 ever and after running 19 intervals! Lee Evans our Olympic record holder 400-meter runner was watching and said "man you guys were flying". That I never forgot and consider his comment an honor coming from such a great. That showed I was in tremendous condition. I had run 1:46.6 the week prior at the NCAA in Knoxville TN. (in 99 degree extremely humid heat) I loved heat and humidity, not chilly cold or even 72 degrees. I still do. But alas I left my race on the practice track and ran a slow struggling 1:51, not my 1:46 potential, and on National Network TV. What an embarrassment.

Second Place 1965 High School District Meet at Proviso West. 1:52.6 880

<u>Sixth fastest time in entire USA High School Runners</u>

RACING AT UNIVERSITY OF ILLINOIS

University of Illinois Open Meet 1 month prior to Big 10 Record-it was a smooth 880 in 1.51.2

Training pays off

First Place 880 1969 Northwestern Record 1:49.1 880

Remember one goal of the short outdoor peak season of mid-April to mid-June is NOT to get injured, stale, or sick from overtraining. It has been a long year of training since the prior July. Maintain your zip, energy, enthusiasm. These are the races that count, that you have been training for all year. Do not mess it up. Race, qualify, and win. You hear?

1962-1971 HIGHLIGHTS

So now I am going to summarize some of the other highlights of my running career with some anecdotes. The end of this book also has the workouts summarized in outline form with a brief discussion about my goals and how I hope to help you become a better runner.

history.

attached from any team, or he may enter law school.

Former EP track star, Ralph Schultz practices on the Northwestern field after tieing the world's indoor track record for the 1,000 yard run at the U of I on March 1.

MATT C. BIRK

Spring Outdoors 1969

READERS NOTES: What do you think about this training program so far?

TIMELINE 1962-1971

This part of the book is about the 10 years I ran track in high school and college and 2 years with the University of Chicago Track Club. I've already talked pretty much about my first year and a half at Evergreen Park High School and a few college race highlights, but here goes.

Fall 1962

So as I said, we had a great cross-country season in 1962. I was extremely motivated and excited. All of us became known around the school. The football team also had a great year, the best in school history. Record 11-0. Ranked #6 in the State of Illinois. Best defense, opponents could hardly score. I remember Neil Stapleton, a defensive end, chasing an opponent ball carrier running around the end, and Neil just dived at him from behind and just caught his foot bringing him down to the ground. This prevented a touchdown. The team was like this. Two players got athletic scholarships to the University of Wyoming. Then basketball season started in mid-November. I was pretty good on the Sophomore team. I had matured and improved my game from my awkward Freshman year. I was the shooting guard. This meant I could shoot but was not a good ball handler. But I could really pass well and set up other players to score. I hustled on defense. I had learned to shoot from all those countless hours and years of practice in my backyard hoop and the local school park. It was great fun playing on Friday nights before big enthusiastic student crowds, the cheerleaders, lighted scoreboards, the time out horns and buzzers, the official announcer, and school dances in the gym afterward. The bus rides to away games as the visiting team, seeing our opponent, their gym, students, and school added to the excitement. I always compared them to my own school. After home games my parents invited my teammates, the parents, the coaches, and a few cheerleaders over to our small house to talk, laugh, and eat Sloppy Joe's (barbecue beef sandwiches). We had an average team, so a win was a big deal. But mostly, the incredibly intense practices and drills, lasting 2 hours, developed my endurance during the long winter in preparation for track season, thank you, Coach Roland Ryan.

Spring 1963

In the Spring of 1963 I began running again with the high school team. Right away I was on the Varsity, a big honor. As a Sophomore I was learning about workouts, but we still ran those 660 yard all out time trials around the school. But I knew there was a better way to train. I walked off 220, 330, and 440 yards and marked off the school sidewalk with chalk. This was for early Spring workouts as a Sophomore and my Junior and Senior years starting in winter (on clear days) from February to April. So I would run interval workouts up and down the ladder, 220, 330, 440 and back down, or 4x220 mixed with 4x440. I was onto something! My best 880 time as a Sophomore was 2:03 down from 2:11 the prior year. But I was still primarily a miler. I won the Conference Varsity Mile in 4:44, which sounds slow, but we weren't great runners in the south suburbs in those days. I probably won by 30 yards, led all the way, even pace, feeling smooth and comfortable. The meet was at Reavis High School. The student's fathers were mostly truck drivers and factory workers, good union men. I remember my mother was there, we went out to dinner afterwards. Two weeks prior to that I was at the State Qualifying District Meet at Proviso West High School. Wow was I stoked with so many great runners there warming up for their important races. This was the ultimate, here I was, in the big time, what I had strived for. I was trying to make the qualifying time of 4:38. My prior best time was 4:45. There were 2 heats, I was in the slower one. But all I remember was I hung in there, pumped up seeing I was competitive. The pace was fast. I ran like heck at the end, all I had. I was chasing Mike Koneisberg from Proviso East. I almost caught him, and lo and behold I ran 4:37.5, I made qualifying by half a second! I was extremely thrilled, as were my parents, friends and of course my coaches, John Megson and Roland Ryan. I had done it! It showed a certain championship quality I was developing that I could race with the best in those highly developed suburban track programs. I didn't even have a time close to that race. My mindset was such that I had to make the State Meet. I was proud of myself and felt I had broken into a special club, a new higher level of performance and expectations. The following week I ran in the State Meet at the University of Illinois, a great thrill. I was in the second heat, a large bunch of runners, and I ran a mediocre 4:44 and finished in the middle of the pack. I was disappointed. The state champ, Larry Wieczorek of Proviso East High School, won in 4:12. He went on to the University of Iowa and became Big Ten Champ. Today he is Director of Track and Field at Iowa. Four years later I would beat Larry in the half mile in 1:54 at a home track meet at Northwestern. What irony! (I think).

The University of Chicago Track Club (UCTC)-- High School Years

The summer came, and now I found out about the University of Chicago Track Club (UCTC) summer schedule, so I went to several of those meets, maybe all of them. There's six of them starting about June 20 to the end of July. There I became acquainted with the big world of track. Chuck Shultz was there from Evanston High School, who was the State cross-country champion and two-mile champion. I met all these different athletes from those big time northern and western suburbs that I emulated so much and respected. And there were numerous college athletes there, and we would run a modified track meet with different events from week to week, 440, 660, 3/4 of a mile, mile, 1.5 miles, and then some of the sprints in the field events. So I loved it. They were Thursday nights at 6:00 so I would drive down there, or my step-father might drive. And it was very, very good memories. That was between my sophomore and junior year, and then between my junior and senior year, and then between senior year and freshman year at NU. But it really was a great training and learning experience for me and enriching to be at that fantastic university

One of the interesting things was that under these giant, old football stands was a sort of labyrinth of offices and rooms, which they had turned into handball courts. But lo and behold, this is where they did the research on the atomic bomb and the Manhattan Project in the early 1940s (the first controlled atomic chain reaction). So there I was of all the ironies of life. That's how it is at The University of Chicago. The track was very unusually shaped. It wasn't as long as the outdoor tracks. It had short straightaways and huge, wide turns. It was packed into and was surrounded by large, 12-foot high stone, concrete walls that had a feeling you were in a castle fortress. And at the one end was the old gym and PE building. It had quite a dramatic look of gothic substance and tradition to it. It was a great place to run. The stadium was named Stagg Field after Alonzo Stagg, the great University of Chicago football coach from 1892-1932. Record 242-112 against top national teams and seven Big Ten Championships. He was an innovator of new plays such as the reverse and man in motion. He coached track for 32 years. He lived for 102 years. Hoorah!!!

So we came to the fall and I ran cross-country. I did well. I was the top guy on the team now. We did pretty good in the conference. We weren't as strong. We may have finished third. I finished second in the conference meet, I remember that. It was at Rich East High School. I near killed myself chasing Rich Roche from Park Forest, Rich East High School. I made it to the State Meet. I did better than the prior year, about 78th. You see it was hard at Urbana down there because the pace was so fast and York High School would take off in a pack, all those green uniforms. And there was a very steep hill you had to run, short and steep, which took it out of me. And then you'd round the turn, and it was about a 440-yard straightaway to the finish. So it was really a hard, long finish. But it was great to go down there and exciting to be by the University of Illinois. I got thrills out of that. And to be with the coaches on an overnight trip, talking and kidding with them. I felt important, with a special star recognition building inside myself.

OLD STAGG FIELD TRADITION GOTHIC WALL WITH IVY

More Basketball

After six, eight weeks of drills and sitting on the bench, not really feeling too much part of the basketball team, in mid-January 1964, Junior year I just quit, and decided to devote my time to track, which is one of the best things I ever did. And what happened is I started doing those outdoor runs I've talked about at the Evergreen Park hilly golf course in the deep snow and in the evenings up and down the crunchy packed snow for those four half-mile hard runs in the evening. In those wintry, beautiful wintry nights.

So that winter of 1964 I started going down there once or twice a week to The University of Chicago Field House to work out, which was fine with Ted Haydon and that group of runners. The University of

Chicago Track Team usually worked out from 3:00 to 4:30 PM. And then all us other track club open athletes started at 4:30 which suited me fine because that's about the time I arrived on the bus from home. And I just started running interval workouts indoors once a week, sometimes twice a week. I also ran some time trials on the weekend. I may have even run an open meet, which was okay because we didn't have an official season until the third week of March. I remember that very well. The fieldhouse was an immense indoor space with a clay 220 track. A 330-yard track would have fitted in there. It would be considered a rustic musty antique now. It was not made for great performance, but it was comfortable for training and preserving athlete's legs. It was also durable for all those 100's of races and relays run there every year. It had a towering gigantic ceiling with huge windows at one end allowing in some rays of dim sunlight. I can't help but wonder if all these wonder synthetic surfaces today are healthy for training despite what the manufacturers and athletic officials say.

And I also remember, I don't know if it was my junior or senior year, something happened to one of our cars, and I couldn't drive down there so I took the bus. Actually, three busses. I left school at 3:00 PM and walked a quarter mile or more to home. Then I walked back past the school to the bus stop about 3:30, hopped on a bus heading north down Kedzie Avenue, which had one switching stop at the Marquette/67th Street substation. It continued on to 55th Street. I had to get off the bus there. I remember very well Talman Federal Savings and Loan in the days when savings and loans were big. Then I had to catch another bus, which was the 55th Street bus, (which went through a tough neighborhood, but no one ever bothered me) which took me quite a ways east, half hour drive perhaps, and let me off a block from the field house at 55th Street and University. Right there at the bus stop was the fire station and then Jimmy's Woodlawn Tap, a famous student and professor hangout, (still there) which I went into later in my life when I became older to relax with other UCTC athletes after meets. It was dark, grey sky, frigid, walking the long block to the field house stone edifice, a gothic like building built perhaps in 1925. The track was clay, the fieldhouse had a musty odor, not brightly lit, but not altogether dim either. It was busy, as if people were conducting their own lab experiments as in the University itself, but on their bodies instead. I was part of a great noble group of athletes molding and shaping their bodies. The talented and less so, just as intense. It made an indelible impression on me. I feel proud to have been a part of it. I was being driven and pulled toward champion status. Most teenagers could never have done this trek twice weekly.

UNIVERSITY OF CHICAGO FIELDHOUSE

So I would walk down to the field house, this big mammoth, old place that's musty inside, with a tremendous amount of history, and a run a track workout with Ted Haydon doing the timing. He gave me some advice, and then of course I kind of did what I thought was right based on my research for myself. And I got to meet all these other athletes and people from all walks of life. John Munger, a counselor at Homewood Flossmoor High School, an older man to me at that time, maybe pushing 30, who was still trying to run as an amateur with mediocre times. There were some great athletes there, college professors, all sorts of people. Most of whom I didn't really know, but I got to know later. Dick King was quite a character. He ran long distance every day at age 40-60 with a distinctive style, a shuffle that amused me. Guess what? That's how I run today, the old man's shuffle. Then there was Ken Young who ran an indoor Marathon in the field house track, 206 laps!!!!. And Pat Palmer, a well-known astrophysics professor (math and computers) who I stay in touch with today, and Jim Corboy with his perpetual smile. And many others. I met Dick Gregory, the famous comedian and civil rights activist and a former runner.

So I tried to condense a workout. It's hard to remember. But I probably ran eight times 220 with a 220 jog rest, probably in the high 20s. Or six 440's in the mid-60s with a 440 jog. And occasionally, probably a hard three-quarters, which Ted Haydon liked. I don't know what the time was, 3:15-3:18 maybe, if that. Sometimes Ted had me run a hard 600 which was a gut wrenching experience. And then I would shower up down there in the old locker room and walk to the bus stop. It was dark. It was bone chilling cold in the 20s. It was pushing 6:00 PM. It was about close to an hour bus ride, depending on the

weather, and when I got home it was pushing 7:00 in the evening. I'd have dinner and do my homework and relax and watch some television. Those shows like *Ben Casey-MD* and *Gunsmoke*. We all remember those if you were in America, I believe. And believe it or not 3 days a week I did exercises in my bedroom for 20 minutes, I wrote all this down in my training manual. Nothing would deter me from reaching my goals.

The interesting part of being in the locker room my junior and senior years when I went down to The University of Chicago for the meets and for workouts is I got to know African-American, black men athletes, talking to them on the track but also just casually in the locker room. There we were changing our clothes, taking showers, and that creates a certain familiarity that we're all alike when you're stripped down out of your clothes and whatever socioeconomic position you have. That was really good for me because there were no black people in my community. And when I went to Northwestern there were hardly any there as well, except some athletes and a few spectacular students on scholarship. So I believe that was a good thing. And I liked getting to know them a lot.

High School Spring 1964

Then we continued on into the spring, Junior year, 1964. I regrouped with the Evergreen Park High School Track Team, and we ran a ton of meets. We'd run meets Tuesdays, Thursdays and then sometimes Saturday relays, the Elmwood Park Relays, different places. So I was running lots of races. But I ran hard workouts on Mondays and Wednesdays because I didn't want to lose the workout time. I didn't rest for those weekday meets. I don't know how I ever did it, but I remember running pretty hard workouts on a soft, cinder Evergreen Park High School outdoor track. In the lousier weather, whenever the track was mushy, we would jog a mile to the Evergreen Park Shopping Center and run sprint and stride workouts of 100 to 200 meters at the end of the shopping mall parking lot in the first level. There was a second level so we were protected from the rain. And on weekday afternoons there weren't that many cars in that particular distant location from the stores.

March of 1964, Junior Year :

That Spring during outdoor season I was maturing as a runner, getting a reputation. And I decided to concentrate on the 880, which is the 800 meters today. I still ran the mile. But in all those meets we ran, those dual meets, which were not like the multi-team meets relays during the week, I would run the

880 first, somewhere in the low two's. Then I'd come back and run the mile and win that as well, probably at 4:48 to 4:55. And then I anchored a mile relay in the low 50's. Then I ran hard workouts on Monday and Wednesday as well so I got in great shape. The workouts were mostly on the track, timed, interval workouts by myself. And occasionally a distance run along the railroad tracks but at the bottom off on one side, or on a path through the prairie, not next to the tracks themselves. That's how it was in those days. Then over to Ridge Country Club and back. Maybe 3-4 miles, pretty slow.

So the season progressed. And then I was really wanting to break two minutes in the 880, and I finally did it at the Dundee Relays on a beautiful Saturday afternoon at the end of April. I ran 1:59.4. And coach Roland Ryan was cheering me on at one turn, "Come on, Schultz, you can do it." And I just pushed that thing and sprinted away and I won the race. It was a big highlight and a beautiful day with probably 25 schools at the meet. The season went on in my junior year, and we had a really good track team. I qualified for the State meet in the 880. I think I ran 1:56.5 at Morton West in the Districts, which qualified for the State Meet. But then I hurt my hip, you know, it tightened up and a little snap in there. You guessed it, running too much speed work before the meet, several days before. I told you that speed kills, injures you. So I did go to State, and I finished fifth in 1:55.5. The injury slowed me down a little bit. I might have run a second faster. But in the final straightaway, at Memorial Stadium at the University of Illinois, Steve Cullinan, who became my teammate and is still my friend passed me and ran 1:54.8. I'll never forget that. And he got offered a scholarship to Northwestern as well to run track. We are in touch today.

ABOVE: Leading Dundee Mile-4:37 after 1:59 880

The next week, four days later was the Conference Meet. I was favored to run the 880. In the last 100 yards, I was running the race and something really popped in my hip-thigh connection by my groin, and I hobbled in, and I ran the race in 2:03. And my teammate Bill Abel just could've passed me easily, and he was running his standard 2:03. And he just stopped, running in place to let me finish. What a great guy Bill Abel was, and he was my teammate, who later went on to Grinnell College and a career at John Deere, the company that makes green tractors. So I won that meet, but I couldn't run the mile relay. And if I had, we would've won the meet. We put an alternate in there, and we almost won. But we lost by a few points, and I was heartbroken. I actually cried, and I was extremely unhappy. But the season was over.

1964 Mile Relay team 3:24.6 State Qualified L to R. Darin Minsky, Jim Vitkus, Bill Abel & Me. The good old days.

That summer after my injury healed, after 5 weeks, it was back to the University of Chicago Track Club summer meets, seeing again all these wonderful people and getting a lot of experience and seasoning under my belt. That was the summer I also worked at my step-father's cousin's supper club, the Red Lantern Inn at 63rd and Ashland Avenue as a bus boy from 4:00 in the afternoon until midnight. And was that a difficult, tense job. I worked very hard clearing and setting up tables for a group of demanding waitresses non-stop. I take my hat off to all people who labor on hourly wages today. They need more income and higher wages and respect.

As I discussed earlier, I also went to the Aqua Park pool every day. I'd ride my bike there. It was a mile and a half each way and I would spend half the day there, sunning, playing in the water, hanging out with my friends, talking to the girls. I got incredibly tan. It wasn't healthy, but we didn't know that in those days. The tanner the better.

Cross Country 1964

My senior year in cross-country, again we had a good team. I was the top runner. And we won most of our meets. And at the Conference Meet, I finished second. Again, I used to kill myself running those cross-country meets. Fred Peterzcak was first from Bremen High School. I also qualified for the State meet, and I did better. I think I finished like, I'm guessing, 48. And York won it again. Those guys were really fantastic, almost surreal. The most highly trained team in the country. It was a beautiful fall day.

I loved to run. The team would go to the forest preserves and run practice races through the forest preserves on Saturday. It was really a wonderful time. An interesting side light: at the Rich Central Invitational in October, I was out near the front of the race. It was about two-thirds finished. It was a new high school. We had to kind of skip over a concrete drain that was about perhaps at most three feet wide with two sides about 4 inches high. And my foot caught on it, and I did a front flip, landed just over it on my hands, jumped onto my feet and kept running, and never missed a beat!

It was probably one of the most acrobatic events of the year, not just for me, for anybody. Quiet amusing, isn't it? So the season ended, and again the State Meet was just an exciting experience. I was just full of awe and wonder and good feelings.

One thing I want to add about cross-country in high school, I was not a natural cross-country runner. And when I ran those really hard meets, Conference, District, State, I really gutted it out (by the we ran 1.9 miles). And by the 1.5-mile mark I was done. I just ran it with guts to be honest with you. I was in severe runner's pain. It was just part of my motivation, and I did well. But it didn't come naturally. But it did me a lot of good. And then again at Northwestern as well, running distance in the fall, which I think some of my half-mile competition didn't do very much of that at all. My best high school 2 mile times were about 9:50-10:20

Well, we ended cross-country, and again now I was <u>not in basketball</u>. So I continued running outdoors as I can remember, three to four miles, three or four days a week. Sometimes on our track, sometimes through the neighborhoods or at the golf course. I got in the habit of driving up to Beverly about two or three miles away, this beautiful Chicago neighborhood full of beautiful, sprawling 1950s style houses. And they kind of looked like old Mafioso homes that you'd see be depicted on TV. A lot of winding little roads, a hill or two, and a forest preserve. I liked it. Anyway, I'd run in and out through those neighborhoods cruising in a natural rhythm. I was in the zone, the flow.

READERS NOTES: Have you run in the ZONE? What's it like?

Indoor 1965

At Christmas time, I ran in The University of Chicago Holiday Meet. I don't recall what I ran, but I probably ran an 880 about two minutes or so, close to it. And I'd do some track running then indoors, eight 220s maybe 28-32, or five 440s at about 58-64 effort. I'd go down there a few times a week. But then in January, school started again, high school. It was sort of a repeat. I would run in that crunchy snow some nights. I'd also shovel snow some nights just as I have said. And I'd go up to the Evergreen Park Golf Course. I'd walk, jog less than a mile up there, and run my 45 minutes of hard striding and speedplay, mostly in the snow. And if there wasn't snow, I still wore those Air Force boots. I was out there recently in the summer, looking at it, and it brought back a lot of memories. Part of the course is flat, and some of it had some short, steep hills that was a challenge to run. I enjoyed that. It was also a challenge to play golf on it. But I also was running at The University of Chicago indoors. I had to keep up with the other Chicago suburban high schools that were in the western and north suburban conference (I looked up to them). So what I did is I would go down to University of Chicago track once or twice a week to run indoor track workouts. Sometimes Rich Freed, our All-State pole-vaulter, would drive down as well with a few other teammates who decided to come along and train. And then I'd run again those eight times 220 workouts, or six times 440, or a ¾ mile and a few 150's at race pace, maybe four. Those type of interval workouts while I was down there. And maybe a mile-and-a-half run indoors for time at 7:30. Sooooo that's what I did. But then there were also meets down there. There were a few open meets, and I could run in them because track season in high school didn't start until the end of March. There were also these Sunday afternoon, I'll call them, time trials for want of a better word. They were track meets, informal. Whoever showed up, they'd have a few events. And Ted would say, "Get ready, get set," boom, and shoot the gun off, and we'd take off and run our distance. I remember running the 660 there. And there was some competition. They'd run about 3:00 PM. Sometimes my step-father would drive me down. And this all helped build me, you know, keeping competitive. I had to do it, and I wanted to do it. It's exciting to be in a major university in their facility when you're a high school kid. You know what I mean, right guys and gals?

READERS NOTES: What type of racing did you do in college? Number of meets and races? It seems to me most colleges don't run in enough meets as we did in the past. Too many off weekends. And the Big 10 Indoor Meet is way too soon. Should be 2 weeks later around March 7th or so. You need meets to get into racing shape. Do you prefer hot or mild weather, humid or dry climate?

University of Iowa **Northwestern University**

Iowa and Northwestern University

I'll tell you an amusing story. Obviously by this time, I was looking at colleges and where I could go to get a track scholarship. I had big ambitions. So still I wasn't that terribly known, finishing fifth in the Illinois State Meet my junior year. Probably through my friend Pete Davis, Northwestern took an interest in me. Coach Bob Ehrhart had come down to visit my parents and I that summer at our home, before my senior year in high school. He really emphasized what Northwestern could do to make me a polished upwardly bound young man. My parents ate that up and it made me think too. So now it was February. 1965. My track coach at my behest had sent out letters to different college track coaches fishing for an athletic scholarship. I had schools interested, a big interest from Iowa where we took a recruiting trip. My coach was friends with the Iowa coach. So my step-father and my coach, we went there for a weekend in the end of January and saw a basketball game. We spent the night in a hotel and met with the coach, and it was good. I eventually got a scholarship from Iowa, which I treasure. I have the letter from Coach Cretzmeyer ("Cretz") in my storeroom. I also got interest from Dartmouth. And eventually, I got a half a scholarship from Stanford, a letter from Payton Jordan, the famous former US Olympic coach, which I have kept in my treasure chest as well. I became impressed by Northwestern my Junior year. Each year the Mustang Varsity athletes were taken on a trip to a NU basketball game and dinner at a Wilmette restaurant. We always had the same thing, big plates of fried chicken covered in honey I loved it. That year I took a walk prior to the game all around a local Wilmette neighborhood. I was so impressed, it was so classy and full of successful people, with beautiful homes.

I knew this was it and I wanted to become a member of the upper middle class. It was unlike anything I ever knew. I BECAME TORN BETWEEN THE CLASSY UPWARD MOBILITY OF AN NU EDUCATION AND THE SMALL CITY BUZZ OF the complex sprawling Big Ten campuses with so many activities and people. By contrast NU was a suburban quiet campus with manicured lawns, somewhat stately and self-confident, with a somewhat homogenous upper-class high achievement student body. I felt a little out of place Freshman year because all the students from wealthy had backgrounds that were different it seemed. In high school no one had parents who were big time bankers, businessmen, lawyers, or owned companies. Maybe that's why my attachment to big corporate business is not so strong, although I understand its benefits.

I just went to a meeting in Evanston with Coach Haynes and Coach Brobst, the Northwestern Women's Cross Country coaches. It was a great time. We exchanged comments about their program and training methods and mine in this book. I believe I gave them some positive encouragement and I felt a nice boost after meeting them. They are building up the program and I truly believe they are capable of winning the Big Ten title within three years. Last Fall in 2018, Aubrey Roberts finished second in the Conference Meet, a tremendous accomplishment. They now have an excellent 300 meter soft artificial grass training oval around the brand new magnificent indoor football practice field. This is better for training and lessening leg stress than any regular indoor hard artificial track surface. It can also be used during the Spring season. Recruits should like it.

MICHIGAN STATE HERE I COME

50,450 students on one campus

I was also interested in Michigan State. I think it had something to do embedded in my mind from the great Duffy Daugherty football teams of the late '50s and early '60s. I was a big football fan, and I used to imagine I was playing for them as a kid. It also had to with the Big Ten large campus, diverse students and ideas. I believe Michigan State has the largest on-campus enrollment of any university in the US, 50,340 students and 600 student clubs. The school was the first USA Land Grant University. I still follow their excellent sport teams. I got admitted to Michigan State in the late fall under their early admissions honors program just individually as a student. And then for the next several months, my track coach tried to contact Michigan State, the coach there, but there was just no interest in me. And they did recruit John Spain, this incredibly talented half-miler, who got injured. So he never really became a rival -- I don't know what ever happened to him. He never came around. But he showed great potential through his sophomore year and was a threat to me. I'll tell you, he would've been the world's greatest half-miler. I would still like to coach middle-distance runners maybe at Michigan State using my methods. I think I could really build up that 800-1500-Mile group to National All-American status. Give me two years. For real.

Jenison Field House Indoors Competed 1967,1968,1969. 1000-yard run record

MICHIGAN STATE SPARTANS (Deep Green color)

I set the Jennison Fieldhouse 1000 yard run records in 1967 and 1968 and ran neck and neck in the mile against Jim Ryun, the American Record holder and Olympian in 1969. Two of my high school friends were students at MSU then. I made friends with a couple of MSU runners so I socialized a little too when I was up there.

Maybe Michigan

Well, I also was interested in Michigan and had received some interest from them. So Don Canham, who was the track coach then and who became the famous athletic director, invited us out, my step-father and I to Michigan for the weekend. We drove out there on a beautiful, sunny, ice cold, end-of-January weekend on a Friday. It's about a four-hour drive, and my step-father had this big, large Ford sedan car. We we came into Ann Arbor, we were put up at the Student Union Hotel. We were on our own that evening and ate there. My eyes were wide open as I wandered around in this incredibly impressive, gigantic University of Michigan campus, buzzing with energy and students going this way and that way, and thinking and feeling how independent I might be some day to be a student there, and what an honor it is to go to Michigan. I was in awe and a little bit intimidated.

Well, the next day, we met Don Canham at his sporting goods school supply store because he also had this side business. And he said coaches don't get paid enough. He had all the large heads of different big game from Africa around the sporting goods walls from his trips to Africa on Big Game hunts. But that didn't bother me then, and it was not an issue. But politically incorrect today. So anyway, we had a nice talk. And then Coach Canham was interested. He said, "If you're interested in law school, Michigan is the best." And he said, "Let's see what happens." This is on a Saturday. And then my step-father and I got complementary tickets to see the track meet, and then we drove home. We got home about 6:00 PM or so Saturday night. And I went out with my friends and went to a party and a dance and kind of wore myself out and slept in Sunday morning, I was hungry and thirsty. So I drove down to McDonald's. And I remember having a fish sandwich and a giant orangeade. And then a few hours later, I drove down to The University of Chicago, and there was one of these time trial track meets around 3:00. They had an 880 so I ran it. There were probably five of us in the race, but I was the only runner of any ability. And so we took off. And I felt great, really smooth and powered up. I ran an even pace all the way. And lo and behold, I ran a 1:54.0 880, which by the way is a 1:53.3 800 meters today. No one behind me. The next guy was probably 2:05. And I had broken my best time by a second and a half from the prior outdoor season at the State Meet. It was just considered like a miraculous sort of thing. I had already run a 1:58 in a time trial at the end of December indoors, in a race with Steve Szabo of Iowa which was very impressive to me and to Ted Haydon. I ran splits of 28, 30, 30, 30 and I passed Steve at the end.

So anyway, I ran this great 880. And then Monday morning, 2 days later, Ted Haydon, unknown to me, called Don Canham at the University of Michigan and told him about it. And by Thursday, I have in the mail a signed letter by Coach Canham on his University of Michigan stationary offering me a full-track scholarship for 100 percent, room and board, tuition and books. Of course, I have that in my treasure chest of memorabilia as well. And I think it's just kind of amusing in the timing and the unlikelihood of that actually occurring and me running so well out of the blue after having such an exciting weekend. That probably is what pumped me up. With no competition. Anyway, that shows what strange things can happen in life.

So I went out and ran a few more meets through the indoor season. And then our season started at the Oak Park Relays. I had run a 4:33 or so the prior year there. And that winter I had run a 4:27 mile down at The University of Chicago Field House as a senior in high school, which was quite impressive. It was probably one of the top four times in the State of Illinois indoors at that date. It was an open meet. I went to the Oak Park Relays with high hopes and competing against the likes of Proviso West's Bruce Bowman and Jim Letterer. I loved Oak Park, with its stately trees and traditional large homes built in the 1920's. Frank Lloyd Wright, the famous architect, designed a home there in the unique swept prairie style. And strangely enough, it was an evening meet. We left early evening. And we were off by an hour, and we missed the meet, the race. I was totally heartbroken. I started crying in the backseat and whining, and it wasn't too mature, but I was just crushed that this opportunity had fallen through my hands.

High School First Place Dundee Relays

Winning mile in 4:37 after a 1:59 880. I ran close to even pace, 68-70-70-69

My Junior Year. Weather was perfect, sunny 72, no wind. I was very fit and in control. I lead both races all the way. Sure was fun.

READERS NOTES:

What is the best way for you to train for the mile?

Summer 2017 Lincoln Park Chicago Lakefront Running with Son. A wonderful place

Spring Summer 1965 Senior Year

Well the outdoor season began, and we entered our flurry of meets. As I have said I would run two or three events. And frankly, I don't know how I did it because I always worked out hard on Monday and Wednesday because you couldn't just run meets without continuous workouts to improve. And I guess that's when you're 17, you have that kind of endurance and strength. I ran workouts by myself and timed myself. And I also ran with two friends of mine, who were also half-milers, Mike Brennoch and

Bill Abel. So in terms of workouts, they were on this soft cinder, dirt track, which is good for training. It's now a beautiful, artificial surface. Again, similar workouts. Like 8x220 intervals, 6x 440, or up and down the ladder, 220, 330, 440, 330, 220, fairly hard, pushing into anerobic capacity. Also tossed in some two mile runs at a pretty good clip. I was getting better at this distance running.

So I gradually improved over this period. And then of course at the big meets, times dropped. At the Moose Heart Relays towards the end of the season. I ran against future Olympic Bronze Medal winner, Rick Wohlhuter, who set a world record in the early '70s. And I beat him. It was a very windy day. At the time, I was about twice his size, that may have something to do with it. But we both ran about 1:53.8. And little did we know that in the future, Rick would become one of the world's top half-milers and known throughout the world. And I would tie a world record as well. I saw him at a recent reunion at the University of Chicago Track Club. It was marvelous to see him. Another runner I respected and feared was Steve Bitner from Homewood Flossmoor High School. He was a great 440 runner and began racing some 880's. One home meet at my high school he ran the 880 against me. It was a tough race. I followed him all the way and down the final 120 yards I strained with all my might and won by a stride in 1:58. Wow! I think the isometric strength training gave me the extra holding power. He could have been nationally ranked in the 880. Steve went on to Yale and then to The University of Chicago Medical School. He is a physician today.

The season continued, and the big District Meet came up. This is the prelude to the State Meet. You have to meet a certain qualifying time to make it down state. Of course, I knew I would make it down state, but I ran against Craig Grant, my rival, who was the best half-miler in Illinois and one of the top five in the nation. We ran at Proviso West High School, which is his home track. I was very nervous. And we went out and ran hard and smooth. Craig ran the first 440 faster than me. I was about 10, 15 meters behind. I closed it somewhat at the end, and I ran 1:52.6, which again is a 1:51.9 800m. Craig was about a second faster. It was the best time I ran in high school and I was number six in the nation that year for United States High School athletes. That actually would've been a pretty good time in the Big Ten meets, in some years would have finished in the top three. So I was on my way. I just was amazed I was there, I was the #6 high school 880-yard runner in the entire USA! And it all happened a step at a time, reaching for attainable challenging goals one by one. Determined to let nothing get in my way. All those different type of workouts had paid off, and I had done it mostly all by myself. Well actually the warm encouragement of my Coach John Megson also went a long way to keeping me centered and confident. Oh let me tell you something. In the summer after my Sophomore year Meggie (Coach Megson) had a terrible appendicitis that almost killed him. I wrote him a heartfelt letter. Then in early Fall when he had recovered he came to our away cross-country meet at Blue Island Eisenhower high School to watch me. I was so touched, tears welled up in my eyes. And how ironic that was that this occurred in Blue Island, the home of my father, Richard Schultz, who I also loved dearly. Both were equally key positive figures in my life. I'll tell you, it makes one think.

After the District Meet, we went to the Illinois State Track Meet the following week. It was extremely windy. I hate running in wind. It was a similar race. Craig took the lead. I followed, and then I closed towards the end. And we both ran about a second slower than at the Districts because of the wind. I think I ran about a 1:53.6 Craig was 1:53. I was getting closer. The Conference Meet was the following week at Oak Lawn High School. I was way ahead, no competition. I ran a 1:54 flat (54-60) and won easily, set a Conference record that never was broken. And then surprisingly enough, a 49 split on the mile relay, which was a good second faster than I had run before, which showed I had some speed and endurance. Great.

Second Place 1965 Illinois High School State Meet University of Illinois Memorial Stadium. In the orange is Rick Wohlhuter, third place and future Olympian Bronze Medal

And here's what's amusing, I already had scholarship offers, track scholarships from Iowa, Michigan, NU, Stanford. And then two days after the State meet on a Monday, we're having dinner at my house, and I get a call from Rut Walter, the head track coach at Wisconsin. They had the best track team in the Conference. And he offered me a full scholarship over the phone. I turned him down because I was committed to Northwestern. He tried to convince me that Wisconsin was a better program, which it was. But I liked the idea of being at an elite school and being a bigger fish in a small pond. My future rivals were at Wisconsin, Mark Winzenried and Ray Arrington. Wisconsin had a marvelous program. They were always winning. But imagine that how far I had come, that I turned down Wisconsin. At the annual athletic banquet I was selected as Athlete of the Year. My picture is still above the entrance to the gymnasium.

T

Start of District Meet 1965 1.52.6 (on right)

Well, the season ended, and I stayed in shape by doing some easy running. Then the University of Chicago Track Club summer meets started. And thank goodness we had those meets, they were such fun and athletes of different abilities came together to run and get to know one another. The first meet in mid-June, I ran the mile down there in Hyde Park. My goal was to break 4:20. And you won't believe this but I ran a 4:19.9. I'll still remember that to this day. I broke it by one-tenth of a second. And I thought there was some significance that I was able to achieve my goal, even by such a narrow margin. And of course, Ted Haydon, the famous coach and wonderful person, timed it. And it was my home away from home, the track at The University of Chicago.

So I went through the summer, and we ran some of those open meets, various events, three-quarters, a 440. And then some time in the summer, probably after the 4th of July, I began to train with Rich Schurke. He was a big, large guy, maybe seven, eight years older and in his mid-20s, who was very interested in track and trained individual athletes. He had a crewcut, flat on top, and a full face with glasses that just stared into your face. Very intense serious expression. He lived on the South Side near me so we trained at Beverly Park, which is a giant-sized park where I used to ice skate when I was little, and my Cub Scout Troop used to meet right across the street, of all ironies. This would be about ten years prior when I was 9. And my friend, Pete Davis would drive all the way down from Evanston, a good hour, hour-and-a-half ride. And John Brunner came down from Arlington Heights, and Joe Mortimer, who was a local Evergreen Park High School runner a few years ahead of me, also ran these workouts. Those are the guys I remember. And when I ran, he yelled in a big booming voice. I was afraid of him. The intensity of his workouts were extreme, I was nervous about doing them. It seems to me for about six, seven weeks, sometime in the middle of July to the first week of September, we'd run there. It must have been twice a week. I can't remember the exact days. I would get over there around 6:30 PM. And we'd work out for an hour and a half. And then I'd come home at 8:00. Everybody would go their own ways. I would stop at Jansen's Drive-In, totally exhausted, and guzzle down a few large orangeades and a big juicy cheeseburger. Jansen's was a family owned place and not part of a chain. It's still there. A lot of Catholic high school kids used to hang out there at 99th and Western. On the other corner was a simple hot dog and tamale stand. My step-dad and I used to go there after dinner about 9 PM for a snack. And then there was the Dairy Queen operated by my track coach, Meggie. It was something of a hangout in the back-parking lot. I used to walk down there at 7 PM for a milk shake. The best. I also liked seeing my coach poking his head out the order window saying hi to me. But the workouts that summer were incredible, and they really did a lot of good for me because I'd never trained quite this hard before. We would run hard intervals, 440 after 440, or 880 after 880, or ¾ after ¾. Many, many intervals for an hour. And it was very exhausting and trying, but I was very pumped up. And we'd run on the edge of the sidewalk in a little dirt path next to the grass, around ball fields and swings in a big, long rectangle. Kids playing sports in the middle. That was about probably a 3/4 mile around or close to it. And so it was a pleasant way to spend the summer. They were in the early part of the evening in the summer before the sun went down, it was still light about 8:00 PM. And there was a real softness to the air. Languid still air. Lots of people outside coming and going. And I was getting in great shape to enter the world of big-time college track at Northwestern University.

But in late August Joe Mortimer and I decided to run the 2-man 10-mile relay competition down at Stagg Field, University of Chicago. Joe had just finished his last year on the Northern Illinois University Cross Country team. This strange event was comprised of two runners taking turns running 440's until each had run 20 of them for a total of 5 miles each. You rested while your teammate ran. And amazingly, we won the relay against lots of competition!! I ran 20 x 440 @ 70 seconds with a 70 second rest interval while Joe ran. I was running very smoothly and in the "Zone" Lap after lap. Wasn't sure I could even finish before the race started yet win it. All that hard interval training with Coach Schurke paid off, it really worked! We were both in the Zone and ran together like a perfectly tuned sports car. I sure was tired and after the race gulped down many sodas.

Typical Evergreen Park home 1964 like mine

BACK TO THE PAST----AGAIN

Summer 2017- a car drive through the Chicago South Suburbs

Okay. We're in Evergreen Park in the afternoon. I was just commenting on things as we drove around that afternoon in August 2017. Merrilyn Sweet, my friend is driving. Merrilyn took a left at the next street. Linda Dorl, another high school classmate came along too. She started a successful advertising business in Detroit, Michigan, part of the Surge. We're around 99th and Central Park. I was looking at the nicely groomed houses here. The impression I got is, you know, it doesn't look any different than it did 50, 60 years ago. But it feels safe. Everything is groomed, and it looks stable. It's just an intuitive feeling that came to my mind, strangely enough. Maybe not exciting.

So that's what I think, it just feels comfortable and safe. But it's the same homes. They're in impeccable condition. Exact same homes. It's like they just sprouted up out of the ground and were reborn. And the trees may be bigger, but it looks the same. There's some little trees. Some big trees. I don't really notice much difference going from a treeless to a large tree neighborhood over 50 years. There's some racially black people here, which we didn't have. Everybody in their nice tidy little homes. And there's a sense of stability here. That's what I said in my last outing. But I'm just saying it again. Compared to some of the other places, it feels safe here. These people are reliable. That's the feeling I have." How about you, Merrilyn? What do you think?

Merrillyn: "I'm surprised that it's the same, as you said. I'd like to go up to one of those houses, maybe one of the houses that I lived in and talk to them to see if they think the same way that I thought 50 years ago".

Ralph: "Yeah, here's the high school. It's, well, the enrollment is down about 30 percent, but it's a strong looking 1950s, '60s type of design. It looks solid, a strong edifice. And everything is neat and clean. Our school had great dedicated teachers from excellent colleges.

Merrillyn: "It looks smaller than it looked then, but the same type of appearance "

Evergreen Park High School-1400 students 1965

Yes. So we're moving now east on 99th Street. And I'm just talking away here, waiting for thoughts to come to me. There's the baseball field, and Merillyn's former house on Utica Ave. Here's the track and field and football field facility. A lot fancier than when I was a student, an artificial professional looking surface. Crossing into my old neighborhood now. Now here the trees look bigger. There's the house that's gone where your friend used to wait for you when you walked home. Slow down. Beverly Madrick's house. Tony the brick layer. Lenny the carpenter. Where's the old Schultz - Chubaty house? There's the Quinlan house. And here's the Schultz - Chubaty house. (Chubaty was my step-father's last name, it's Ukranian). We put a fence up there where I used to play in the vacant lot. Both baseball, whiffle ball, and bouncing a golf ball off the side of the house to practice fielding. On long warmer summer nights a bunch of us would play badminton. There's the house, 2911 W. 99th St. There it is. I grew up in the front there. Take a right. I'll show you where a friend lived.

Ukrainian Orthodox Church Beautiful Icons Step-Grandfather attended in Chicago

All right. We're on Francisco, heading down along the road I used to run on those crispy winter nights. The house on the right corner is the old house. It's still there. That little, tiny house. Look at it. I'm surprised it's still there. The family was working class, very moderate income. The opposite of my classmates later at Northwestern University. The street had a rural small-town look to it in the past, vacant lots, small frame houses mostly. We played ice hockey there after school, pretended we were pros. Oh there's the Esposito place. They had a GTO Pontiac in 1966, a real hot fast car, full of chrome, a gigantic engine. Wow.

Well, we continued on down 99th Street, heading east into Chicago and into Beverly, which is a beautiful area. One of the more well-to-do parts of Chicago. It's full of woody areas and some hills and a Frank Lloyd Wright house. I used to run through there. It was exciting and connected to the forest preserve. I loved running through this different area of winding roads, unique streets, while sprinting and striding and running. I wonder what the people looking out the window thought. But to me, in high school, and then on vacations while in college, it gave me a sense of wonder and adventure and exploration. Similar to when I was a youth in the South Side of Chicago. That theme runs throughout my track career. Sort of a sense of awe in the environment I'm running in, the neighborhoods and what's happening in my life in terms of track and my future life out of college.

That evening we went on to meet Mike Rogalski, my high school friend, who I very much always liked. We had a great dinner eating steaks and pasta in a fancy Italian steakhouse and talked about old times. Merrilyn was there too. It's strange how decades go by but yet you feel as though you've known each other since yesterday. He is also part Russian. He needs to visit Moscow (WITH ME)

MIKE ROGALSKI AND ME IN CHICAGO 2018

READERS NOTES: What do you know about Chicago?

P.S. Two of my men classmates went to West Point the US Army Academy, and The Naval Academy. The prior year another two graduates also went to The Air Force academy and The Naval Academy. That is outstanding. Just think, 4 out of 200 men graduates or 4% admitted to such selective and prestigious schools. Wow.

\

NORTHWESTERN UNIVERSITY 1965-1968

Deering Library 1968

So when we started at Northwestern in the fall there are certain highlights I remember. That's the year the Northwestern University Cross-Country team won the Conference Championship in the Big Ten and went on to finish second in the NCAA National Cross-Country meet at the University of Kansas as I have discussed. Now freshmen weren't allowed to compete then. But I could run the workouts, and they really were impressive. I couldn't believe how hard they looked. How could I ever do them? We used to run workouts at several places. The one I remember was Wilmette Country Club or Golf Course. There weren't quite as many golfers in those days. So when we would run was mostly in October and we

started about 4:00 in the afternoon. We could run on the edge of the fairway in different loops. We ran 20 times 440, or eight times 880, or four times one mile, or three times a mile and a half. These were hard interval runs. I remember being somewhat behind but running respectable for a freshman. I was back there with Steve Cullinan, maybe running interval miles at 5:20 to 5:30, whereas the pack was out there in that 4:40 to 4:50 range. Pete Davis, Craig Boydston, Lee Assenheimer the Big Ten Champ, John Duffield (who is a Rhoades Scholar and now is a political science professor at the University of Montana), Pat Edmondson, they really impressed me. I couldn't understand how anyone could run so far so fast. So I remember that quite well. And there's also a niceness in the fall air. The weather is still warm late in the afternoon but just a little crisp. And it was quite comfortable to run those workouts on grass. We also would run at a place called the Skokie Playfields, which is a giant recreational area in Winnetka with a big golf course and giant open fields. It was adjacent to the Chicago River North Branch and the forest preserves where horses would go through these wide cinder paths. We used to run around the field a few times and up and down the path for several miles. It was about a six-mile run. I enjoyed running through the woods and down the cinder path. We would be hauling pretty fast. Of course, I wasn't up at the front with our top runners. But I would come in there hard at the end. And so we'd have a good workout and cool off at the end. There really is an exhilarating feeling to be running hard for 6 miles, capable, confident, extraordinary, purging one's body and soul. And did I tell you about the runner's high? That great sublime calm warm feeling after a good run that lasts a few hours. No need for artificial stimulants. Kind of nature's reward for a good effort. I still get them. So we went back and forth in two or three Northwestern University station wagons, those big, old honkers from the late mid-'60s. And we'd get home at 5:30-ish and shower and clean up, and then I'd head out to study, and for dinner as well. A hard but satisfying routine. We also ran 4 lengths of the beautiful one-mile long Wilmette Beach. At one end was a short steep hill we sprinted about 6 times. During my Senior year in high school my friend and future fraternity brother (Delta Tau Delta), who had introduced me to Northwestern invited me up to NU my Senior year on an athletic recruiting visit to look at the impressive campus and attend a fraternity party. Of course they fixed me up with one of those beautiful charming NU coeds (girls) and what a great party! Right then and there I knew college life at NU was for me. I remember staying at Pete's beautiful large Victorian Evanston home in the summer a few times. It was soooo comfortable and traditional. I had never seen homes or been inside homes like this before. It had a screened in porch all along one side. Pete would take me out on these hard runs through Evanston out to the high school and back. Maybe some striding along beautiful Lake Michigan. I remember eating peanut butter sandwiches for lunch his mother had made and Pete's favorite snack---potato chips. My

Freshman year he used to haul me out of bed at 7 AM for a hard 3-mile morning run through the Evanston tree lined streets. I didn't like that I'll tell you, but it did me good. Another time he, Craig Boydston, and I went on a workout during a steady light rain. We ran for 30 minutes south of the campus in a nice park full of trees and grass next to Lake Michigan around a pond there. And I wore a plastic knee length clear rain coat and a small fishing hat! I looked like a commuter chasing the train for work. That morning route west of the campus became another favorite place for me to run 3 miles fast and smooth on off days. I loved to look at the homes and wonder what the people were like. A very comfortable feeling.

And boy, did I ever study hard. Between the discipline of track, going to school and studying in the evenings, it really was a rigid schedule. And I don't know how I did it frankly. I couldn't do it again. I threw in a little bit of fun stuff with fraternity activities and football games. But my freshman year I lived in the dorm. And believe it or not, a future famous actor, Peter Strauss, was in my dorm. It was quite interesting. He went on to do some big TV series shows, like Rich Man Poor Man and Masada. I really enjoyed that period of time, getting to being away from home. I was free! And independent at last. My dorm window overlooked Lake Michigan and a small beach there. The sense of freedom and exhilaration was great that I didn't have a curfew. I could go out to dances or a date or out for a hamburger in the evening and not be concerned about coming home. It just was an exhilarating period and also was intellectually exhilarating because I was learning about history and economics and political science and the things I enjoyed, opening my mind to new ideas in a very exciting time in the United States at the beginning of the Vietnam War and the protest movements and the changes in the society, the rebellion of authority, the more intellectualizing of the students in challenging the standards that had developed after World War II in the 1950s, as the USA developed into a commercial and industrial powerhouse. Now it was time to break out of those old molds. Oh yes it was.

One of the ironies is between the several hard practices in the summer with Rick Schurke and the hard fall runs with the cross-country team, I got into tremendous endurance shape. I bet I had more endurance than any of my competing half-miler competitors at the other Big Ten universities. In January indoors at The University of Chicago Open Invitational, I ran a 9:20 two-mile run, even pace. With some focus and additional competition and hard training into March (6 weeks later) I probably could have run 9 minutes and would have won the Big Ten 2 mile that year or come close. In fact, Dick Sharkey of

Michigan State won the indoor 2 mile in 9:02. That was just the beginning of the season. So it's amazing a guy like me, a half-miler of large stature, 6'1", 180 pounds, could run endurance that fast, probably capable of running 2 miles in the 8:50's! But I had this lung capacity. And I had trained to form a tremendous strength base, which was my key to success and what my training program that I'm discussing here with you is about. But remember, my base was not based on doing high grinding mileage. It was a mixture of smooth running and novel intense workout runs with zeal and feeling.

It's hard to remember in the spring. I ran in a few meets here and there. Freshmen weren't allowed to compete in those days-just study they said. But as the spring went on, there was less for me to do in track, but I did workouts without much zeal. And I remember I finally did one 880 time trial all by myself in May at Northwestern University to see how I could do even without competition. And I ran a 1:54 flat, (1:53.3 800 meters) , which was pretty good. It was just slightly slower than I had run the year before in the State Meet so I had managed to maintain some semblance of conditioning. But it still was deflating and I began to doubt my ability. I had lost my edge and toughness. So then we went on to the summer. That summer I worked in the Wildcat Club. I was a counselor to all these youngsters in grammar school who on a daily basis came to Northwestern to play sports and different games. We would pick them up in the morning and play all day. Now I wasn't that crazy about it. In fact, I didn't get rehired because it was kind of boring to me, and I'm not sure I was so good dealing with all these little kids. But I stayed in the fraternity that summer in a room. It was blazing hot. No air conditioning. And I can remember like late at night, 11:00, 12:00, trying to sleep, and I couldn't. So I would go out and take runs through the streets of downtown Wilmette and back at very fast pace. That would be about a three-mile hard run. And I'm surprised the police never picked me up. But, you know, in those days, crime was not such a big deal. And I suppose they felt I was just some kid out running, which I was. In later years I heard that in our fraternity house, a guy named Bill Murray spent the summer there before he became a famous actor. I don't remember him too well. But remember Bill Murray now? *Ghostbusters*, *Caddyshack*, *Stripes*, all these, *Saturday Night Live*. A great actor. I'd like to meet Bill someday. If you're out there, Bill, give me a call, send me a letter. I'm on Facebook. Ralph Schultz

Okay. So in any event, that summer went by, and it was very hot and languid. I liked Evanston. I did some socializing with that North Shore crowd, different than my high school. A friend of mine, Chuck Falk, and I hung out together, who also worked in Wildcat Club summer camp for kids. Chuck was from a small Illinois town, Galva, Illinois. His brother, Rich, was a great NU basketball player, a great shooting guard, set a record of 44 points in one game. And no 3-point shots then or he would have been over 50 points. I saw him play. Both were members of my fraternity, Delta Tau Delta.

Now we get into sophomore year. I was on the cross-country team. We had lost Assenheimer and Boydston, our two top runners, who had graduated. But we still had a core of good runners. I probably moved up to the number four man at this point in time. We had Duffield, Edmondson, Davis, Doug Williamson (Illinois State Cross Country High School Champion), myself, and runners Rich Boudreaux, Bob Hinshaw, and Steve Cullinan. I just spoke with Rich after 48 years. He lives in London after a fine career in Journalism. And what did we mostly talk about? Track and running of course!

So we had a decent team, but we ran a mediocre season. But I remember the Big Ten meet at Wisconsin. Oh do I ever.

Fall 1968 Wilmette Golf Course Cross Country Big 10 Meet

I remember that Big Ten Meet at the University of Wisconsin. I was really nervous. It was my first Big Ten Meet of any kind. And of course, I wasn't the world's best cross-country runner, but I tried. And it was a longways, four or five miles in those days. High School Cross Country was a short 1.9 miles. So the top runners would break 20:00 and 24:00. And probably in those days, that year, I may have run close to 21:00 for four miles and about 26:30-27:30 for five, but maybe slower, especially in this race, the Deep Freeze. But we went up there. It was a bitterly cold early November morning at the rolling Edina Country Club. It was a hilly golf course. It's a beautiful place, but it was freezing cold. It must have been in the upper 30s F. For 2 miles I ran out behind the pack but I couldn't keep up. Between the early fast pace, the exhausting hills, and the icy cold air on my frozen legs I just tightened up and struggled through 5 miles. It was just awful. I just froze out there. I hate running in cold weather. I am a warm weather person. I thrive in hot humid weather. And of course, we wore just those short shorts and jerseys and maybe a T-shirt underneath and light gloves. I didn't finish last, but I was pretty far back. And I actually was disappointed. I thought I could've done a little better. A hot meal afterwards never tasted so good.

You know to run 5 miles in 27:30 is a 5:30 mile pace without stopping. That is pretty good for any human being in the entire world. So when you think about it, us Cross Country runners are a rare breed, capable of training and pushing our bodies way beyond the normal healthy average person's running ability. To be able to take off and run 5 miles at a smooth steady pace is a real gift to be thankful for. It really is. Most people can't do it.

The season ended. I remember running in a Turkey Trot 10K Thanksgiving Day race with 300 runners. My step-father picked me up at the Northwestern dorm and drove me to Mount Prospect, Illinois, a distant suburb, to run and then we went home for a nice Thanksgiving holiday in the fall of 1966.

Wintertime, in January, we came back and began indoor season. I was starting to show some signs of prominence and getting a little more glory again. I remember the Michigan State Relays in old Jennison Fieldhouse. I ran 2:13.6 for the 1,000-yard run Invitational Race. And I won. I set a field house record. It was very exciting going up to Michigan State, which I've always loved and I still do. It's a favorite kind of place to compete. Lots of athletes and spectators (as I remember) and bright lights, a real buzz. I just love the campus with the Cedar River running through it. As I said, I got admitted there as a Freshman on an academic basis. And I might have gone there if they'd given me a track scholarship, but they didn't. I did a lot of my intervals with our walk-on athletes. We became friends, seemed to be some brotherly connection for some reason. Bob Brandon, Webster Groves, Missouri, ran the 440 in 51, Chuck Cox from Minneapolis, Minnesota ran the 880 in 1:56, and Bill Larson, Franklin Park, Illinois ran 1:55 for the 880. He was on a wresting scholarship. He wrote poetry, but sadly died in an accident his Junior year.

The season went on and I went to the Big Ten Meet. And here's something sad but funny. It was at the University of Wisconsin again indoors. I was really excited. We stayed at the Edgewater Inn, this nice, out-of-the-way hotel on Lake Mendota about three-quarters of a mile from the main campus. So I was always excited about exploring campuses and universities and even some of the academic areas, with a sense of adventure, like I had in my childhood. So a friend of mine from the team and I walked all over the campus that day and stopped at some student place for lunch and looked at the students. And we walked up this big hill in the middle of the academic area called Beacon Hill. It must have been a couple blocks long, pretty steep, with the campus academic buildings along each side. I must have walked up there once, maybe I did it twice. But all I know is at the preliminary run the next day on Friday night, I was just beat. My legs had no life, and I was probably ranked third. A University of Michigan runner just whizzed by me at the end in the last turn. I didn’t make the finals by a step. Very disappointing. It just goes to show you, you don't do crazy things like that the day before a meet. It really wore out my legs, period. A lesson learned. A hard one.

Now it was 1967, I was really immersed in school. I really enjoyed it, taking courses in economics and a lot of US history and world history courses and political science, which is what I really liked. And Northwestern was a beautiful campus. I had developed a personal life, made friends, had a girlfriend, Robin. She was a big supporter of the track team, even organized a girl cheering squad. Her family had a large farm estate in Wisconsin and were expert horse (equestrian) people, did summer horse show events like on TV during the Olympics. They even had a fox hunt. Once I followed Robin on a training run. She was on horseback and we went 3 miles through woods and fields with me running right behind at a quick pace. Robin was just amazed. And I remember the spring, I again was considered one of the better Big Ten runners but not the best. I always was looking at the results on the weekend as we went through April into May to see how I ranked. It was a nerve-wracking time. We ran a lot of interval workouts on the outdoor cinder track inside Dyche Stadium. In the middle of April, the football team had spring training for two weeks. They seemed so important running drills and plays on the football turf as we trained running around them on the track. I always wondered if they thought we were crazy. What I remember then is that I finally I broke through to a higher performance level that had eluded me since high school. Two years had passed since my outstanding performances in the State Meet as a Senior in high school. I hadn't really run really well. It might had been good enough for some, but for me, I wasn't in really super shape. So at the end of March into the first couple weeks of April, I did some really hard endurance interval workouts. I remember about the third week, the middle of April, we went up to the University of Minnesota for a dual meet. We flew to this meet, and that was a big treat because we flew to only a few of the meets. And it turned out to be one of those beautiful spring days in the 60s, sunny, no wind. And I finally broke through. I finished second in the mile in 4:14. I won the 880 around 1:51 to 1:52. And I ran about a 49-mile relay anchor. So I had three really good races. And finally, I began to show what I could do. My potential started coming to the surface. I could feel it inside of me. About time. Whew! This was fortunate because the prior week the team flew down to the University of Missouri for an important meet in nice warm southern weather where good race results were likely. I had moved into the fraternity house which was noisy sometimes on Friday nights, when we had a party. So I went to sleep at my friends' dorm that night, but didn't tell anyone. So you guessed it, the alarm didn't go off on time and I missed the plane! I was so upset and disappointed. The coach didn't leave the ticket at the airline airport counter, so I couldn't fly down on the next flight to St. Louis. No e-tickets in those days. And no cell phone!

A week or two later, at the end of April, we all went to the Drake Relays. It was a great thrill. And I remember running the anchor on the sprint medley relay team, which was two 220s, a 440, and then an 880. I set my all-time best, an impressive 1:48.3, the fastest in the Big Ten Conference and a good national time. I finally showed that I could run with the best. It was really exciting because there were hundreds of athletes there from the Midwest, the Great Plains states, many of the best runners in the United States. And the weather was nice. It was warm. And it's in Des Moines, Iowa, every year, at Drake University. A great tradition.

So I felt as though I was ready to run well, and I continued with the outdoor workouts. A little bit more speed training as a sophomore, but I had the training base. We went to the Big Ten Meet at Iowa. It was a beautiful sunny weekend. A nice long exciting car drive with the team. I was ranked second behind Ron Kuchinski from Michigan. And I remember the night before the meet going out to dinner with my parents to a good steak food restaurant. Storing up the calories. And I ran right behind Ron Kuchinski all the way until about the last 220. Then I made my move, and I beat Ron. I ran a great time, 1:49.1, (1:48.4 800m.). Ron was about a half second behind me. It was just a tremendous feeling of glory and fruition that finally I had cracked my best individual time by three seconds and was a Big Ten Champ! So I was one of the best runners now, not only in the Midwest, in the country. So it moved me into the big time. I was very thrilled. I had a great time at the University of Iowa that weekend, because I really always liked being on those Big Ten campuses. I think I went to a fraternity dance with my NU girlfriend. And I particularly had a soft spot in my heart for the University of Iowa, where I had almost chosen to go instead of NU.

Well, as it turned out, we had another big meet called the Central Collegiates up in Marquette University a week or two later. About 30 Midwest schools were there. I think I finished fourth. I just couldn't keep up with the pack. I ran about a 1:50.5, a little off my best and behind John Spain of Michigan State in 1:48. But I had qualified for the NCAA meet in the middle of June held at Brigham Young University in Provo Utah. But unfortunately, as I warned you, I did some really hard speed work towards the end of May, some hard 220s, probably pushing them about 25, which is fast for me if you run three or four. And I popped a little muscle in my hip area, groin. It was a nagging injury. So I went out to Salt Lake City for the NCAA, but I didn't make the finals. I ran about a 1:51, and I was injured. I just didn't have it. I was running without full power. But it was really exciting to be out there. We were there for five days. I remember the day after, or maybe it was two days after the race I took a long hike up those mountains behind Brigham Young University. It was several hours. I walked up along the creek bed, literally to the top of the mountain where I was slugging it out at the top in snow and mud on those peaks. And it was just totally amazing I could do something like that. It's probably up around 10,000 or 11,000 feet. I drank water out of a stream and kept my eyes open for bears and mountain lions. Again, it was that sense of adventure that started in childhood in Chicago. So the season ended, and it was June of 1967.

I went back home to Oak Lawn. My parents had moved there now next to Evergreen Park. I got a job as a stock boy at Wayne's Town Liquors where my dad bought his liquor refreshments. This was a big liquor store on the far South Side of Chicago next to Evergreen Park and Beverly. It was a very hard job.

I didn't like it. I worked from mid-afternoon to evening and all day Saturday, stocking alcoholic beverages on shelves, marking the price and taking shopping carts full of alcoholic refreshments to people's parked cars on Saturday who were getting things for the big weekend parties. I couldn't wait to get home, exhausted. It was a real letdown after being the Track Champ, the first of many letdowns to come. I remember I did run some summer meets at The University of Chicago on a casual basis. I think that's also when I started running once or twice a week at the Palos Forest Reserves on those isolated paths, through that beautiful forest area.

But then Expo '67 was on in Montreal. So that was in August. I quit my job, and I took a trip there with Bob Brandt, my friend, who was about 20 years older than me. He was an intellectual guy. We had a great time. We drove there in his big Cadillac. I was just in awe of all the wonderful worldwide futuristic educational exhibits at Expo '67 and thinking about my future after Northwestern, about working in the international area in some kind of federal government job. I remember it was in Montreal, which is French, along the beautiful and wild looking very wide St. Laurence River. The subway underground trains had rubber wheels. Very quiet. How advanced. And in Chicago the trains screeched so loud your ears were ready to explode. We stayed at a French lady's house. We rented a room. I remember that's when we also discovered Molson Ale, a very tasty drink, that I had at the end of the day at a men's tavern with a long wooden bar, just like in Europe. I just loved it up there along the St. Lawrence River. It was really a different climate and culture. It was a fantastic experience to say the least. I was very curious about the world and what made it tick. I asked Bob a million questions. My future was right there just in front of me. I was pumped up, yes I was.

Northwestern Fall Term didn't start until the end of September. We got there about a week before classes started for the cross-country team. We started late in that beautiful fall weather up along Lake Michigan with the beautiful City of Evanston and Wilmette right there. The big green trees lining the streets. Evanston is a very intellectual kind of community. Evanston was diverse. Wilmette is the upper-class executive, managerial type. A beautiful 1-mile long beach and the otherworldly immense B'hai Temple were there. But the strange part is in early September, The University of Chicago used to have a six-mile cross-country race in Washington Park. It was six one-mile loops called the Six Mile Handicap Run. So Ted Haydon, based on what he thought you could run, would give you a handicap. And so therefore you got to start ahead of other runners. And my handicap might have been two minutes. But nobody realized what good shape I was in. And lo and behold, I won. And I think I ran six miles between 32 and 33 minutes (my actual running time), which is pretty darn good for a half-miler. Everybody was amazed that I won this thing. And I was so excited that I got out into the lead and just kept it up and held the pace. We would run on some small, little bridges made of stone over the lagoon there in Washington Park in this historic place. And it was just absolutely exciting. It was 4 miles from where I lived when I was a boy. Jackson Park Hospital, where I was born, was 2 miles south in another direction on Stony Island Avenue. Strangely, down the street from the hospital eventually was located Operation Push, the African-American Civil Rights group and charitable organization started by Jesse Jackson, the famous black activist and civil rights leader. Nearby also was the Black Muslims Temple, led by Louis Farrakhan. I like that I was born there and not in a white upper-class neighborhood. Part of my circle of life I guess, preordained, who really knows?

The Fall of '67, it was another cross-country season, running the same type of workouts that I'd done before. We had a mediocre team with some probably finished about sixth in the Big Ten that year. The meet however, it was at Northwestern University at my favorite Wilmette Country Club. I ran the best cross-country race of my life. In fact, maybe the only really good one. It was the beginning of November, a nice, beautiful 63-degree, sunny, calm, fall day. I went out and I finished 30th out of 70 runners. I ran a 25:52 for five miles, which was very good, and about 30 seconds faster than my prior best. I remember Roger Merchant, who was my friend at Michigan State, he was a half-miler too. And we ran even the entire race. But then about the last three-quarters of the mile, I just took off. I had a lot left, and I ran a great race. I have a picture of it. It's in the book. So that was a lot of fun. And that's how that season ended.

There is nothing like running down a freshly cut green smooth golf fairway in 70 degree Fall weather.

Me finishing hard Cross Country Meet at Northwestern 1967--5 miles-#30 @ 25.52

As we got into December 1967, my Junior year, I ran at The University of Chicago Holiday Indoor Meet, which they still have. Then I ran the indoor season on the NU team. I remember going back to the Michigan State Relays, and I won again and broke my record time by running a 2:12.8, 1,000-yard run, finished first. I went out and took the lead, running a steady smooth dominating pace. It was all very glorious and lots of fun. I thoroughly enjoyed running in Jennison Fieldhouse in front of all those people and bright lights. I have to tell you that being out front in a race, outcome uncertain, feeling your body respond to all that training, and then realizing you have a lot left and may win, is a real pure instinctive feeling of triumph, perhaps touching a place inside that comes from way back, in man's early development.

I was really coming around then into my own. I was starting to focus on the 1,000-yard run. The week before the Big Ten meet, we flew to Ohio State University and I won the 1,000 down there in, I think, a 2:08.7 time, which is very good. Then we went down a week later for the Big Ten meet. We flew down there. And I won in 2:09.1, which was a new Big Ten record, and I was very thrilled. It was a culmination

of a great season. Yes, I did love the fame and attention. It had become my addiction. And why not? I had earned it. Nothing would stop me now.

So that spring I was really starting to run well. We went out to the Drake Relays again. And I ran the sprint medley relay again on the 880. And who was my competitor? Jim Ryun, the great Kansas miler and world record holder. We ran about even, me a few steps behind. With 200 yards to go I passed him and he just slipped by me at the finish. And we both ran about a 1:48.2. I didn't lose any ground, didn't gain any ground, stayed right with him all the way and it was very exciting. My teammates thought it was great that I could keep up with this world record miler. And that was the highlight of that Drake Relays, which was always an exciting meet. As a team we ran 3:19 and just missed the finals. A fast time. Me, Hoffman, Carlson, and Janulus.

I remember in that season a week later, (I have a film of this) a week before the Big Ten Meet in early May, I ran what used to be a race, a 660, which is one and a half laps on an outdoor track. I ran that in 1:17.4, finished first, the best time in the Big 10. I came from behind. I passed Steve Cullinan, who was leading the race from Northwestern, and then Roger Frasier, this tall, lanky 46 second 440-yard runner from Iowa. I passed him in that long 120 yard final straightaway because I had strength and endurance and could hold pace. And Roger had speed. I believe running those all out 440's in the snow in Air Force WW II heavy pilot boots at the golf course in high school just may have made the difference. Hey, is that an officially endorsed USA Track and Field Federation training method?

READERS NOTES: What do you think about running in combat boots in the snow? And these hills hard? How about in 1 foot of snow?

Above: Me and Larry Wieczorek from Iowa. Beneath: Coach Ehrhart

Northwestern Track Staff

Robin Ehrlich Assistant Manager, Rich Christopher Manager

Finishing stretch of 660 yard run-1:17.4 The 440 split was 51.6-final 220 25.8

Carl Frazier of Iowa in second. May 1968 at Northwestern

The Big Ten Outdoor Meet was up in Minnesota. And unfortunately, it was one of those May weekends where a cold front had hit, and it rained. And they had a cinder track in those days. And it was cold. I made the finals. But the next day, I'm not sure I warmed up enough or maybe because of the cold and rain the day before, and the track was very soft. I had a terrible race. I ran about a 1:51.7, and I think I finished about seventh out of eight or nine. It was just very disappointing. I had one of my off days so to speak. And then a week later, we ran the Central Collegiate Meet. I had another off day. I was tired out. I was getting stale. I ran about another 1:50.5 and finished in the top six in this major Midwestern meet with all sorts of universities competing. I was tired, but I was looking forward to running the NCAA meet in Berkeley, California. The strange part is I had run a great 880 as a relay split and a great 660. Outdoors, I hadn't run a good 880 individual race yet. In fact, I hadn't run it that often.

So I went up to the Western Michigan Relays at the end of May. This was my last chance to qualify for the NCAA. I was very nervous because everything was on line. It was a meet of numerous schools, but it was not considered a big meet. I remember going up there- just myself, the coach, our manager Tippy Dye Jr., and a few other athletes. This was it, do or die as they say. I ran the 880. I just barely qualified. I won. I think I ran about a 1:50.4 (1.50.9 to qualify). So I qualified for the NCAA meet in Berkeley, California, three weeks later. I was extremely thrilled to go out there. And relieved.

The interesting part of this story is that of the 40 or 50 of the 880 runners that qualified for the meet, I had one of the slowest times. I had barely made the NCAA qualifying time. We flew out to Berkeley. I absolutely love Berkeley. I loved it there, and I wanted to live in San Francisco. My coach and I went to Fisherman's Wharf to eat one day and drove around town and went to Stinson State Park in Marin County to see the beautiful Pacific Ocean crashing in. So I was in Berkeley, I did fantastic. I finished third and was All American. We had to run three 880s in a row on Thursday, Friday, Saturday for qualifying. And I ran them all in the 1:48s, which would be 1:47.5 to 1:48.2 in the 800 meters. I won the first race, dominating it. The second run, I was in the top three. I made the finals and finished 3rd third. *And I remember what Ted Haydon said before the races, "Ralph, make sure you shake out (easy warm up) early in the morning after breakfast and take a 15-minute easy jog," which I did. And I think that made the difference because then I was not tight during the races. I broke a light sweat and cleaned out the waste products from my body, the lactic acid from my system*. Thank you, Ted Haydon. So for the final at Berkeley, we had one heck of a race. And coming down the back stretch, I cut to the inside. There was a little space between the curb and Ray Arrington, my rival from Wisconsin. We sprinted down the finish. I leaned forward, and I beat him by less than a tenth of a second. It was a photo finish because they announced him as third and me as fourth. My coach protested. They looked at the film, and they switched us. So I was third. And I was All American in one of the better times in the country. I was extremely excited. It was the fruition of a great career and 7 years of training and competing. I have always had a warm place inside myself about Berkeley to this day. Anyone want to offer me a job in Berkeley? Or invite me over? Below: University of California Berkeley Campus

LOS ANGELES COLISEUM PRE-OLYMPIC MEET

When I went back home and flew back to Los Angeles two weeks later, we all ran in a pre-Olympic meet. I wouldn't call it a try out, but an exhibition in the LA Coliseum, where they had the Olympics in 1984 and the University of Southern California plays their football games today. Very very impressive. Olympic flags were flying over this historic mighty stadium. I made a mistake there. I ran about a 1:48-something in the preliminary and made the final. But afterwards at the Coliseum, I ran into an old friend of mine, Craig Schaeffer, from high school. Hadn't seen him in five, six years. I spent a half hour talking to him after the race. My step-father came running out of the stands and told me to get going and loosen up. And I did. I warmed down. But I think it was too late because the next day I just died, and I think I finished last about eighth, about 1:50-1:51. I just didn't have it. I didn't get all the lactic acid waste flushed out of my system the day before. The competitors were terrific. I remember them well. They were just a tough bunch of runners. And so that ended. My parents were out there. So we had a nice time visiting friends, family, and enjoying Los Angeles. I flew back to Chicago

RUSSIA

Red Square Kremlin in MOCKBA (Rus Cyrillic spelling). St. Basil Cathedral in background

The center of the Russian Government.

Red Army Star 1979—both pictures beautiful in color

TRIP TO RUSSIA 1968 AND SOME HISTORICAL ISSUES

I was officially invited to the Olympic try-out camp at South Lake Tahoe that summer to prepare for the Mexico Olympics. There were about, I think, 12 of us in the 880, maybe 14. I guess officially I was ranked about 7th overall in the USA. The idea was to acclimate to the 7300 foot altitude in Mexico City and as well as to prepare generally for the Olympics, and for the try-outs, which were going to be held in the beginning of September. I had a dilemma. I had been accepted to go with the Northwestern University (my school) Russian Department for a study trip to the Soviet Union for 6 weeks in mid-summer (2 weeks in Leningrad, 3 weeks in Moscow, and then 8 days in Lithuania, Warsaw, Berlin, and London.). I decided to go on that trip. Why, folks? Because I didn't think my odds of being the top three to make the Olympic team were that good. I really wanted this trip to Russia because I was interested in Russia, international politics and issues. International Relations was a central field of interest of mine for a career. It was just a marvelous trip. We (a group of about 20 students and 3 professors) went there and flew a part of the way on the Russian airline, Aeroflot, into Leningrad one morning. And I still remember this. The plane landed, it might have been a smaller airport or off to the corner. And we got off. It was 6:00 in the morning, cool, a little hazy, foggy. And right there on the runway next to the plane there were five Russian bureaucrats or agents waiting for us, all dressed very drab, in the same style gray trench coats, not smiling. I think three men and two women. And basically, they looked us over and looked through our suitcases to make sure we didn't have any religious materials, and you're only allowed so much money, dollars that is. Their official welcome was very austere. And I guess that's the Soviet Union for you. We took a bus to a town about 20 miles outside of Leningrad where we stayed at a Workers' Resort. Now this was not a resort the way we in the West think of it. It was basically like a college campus. It was an area full of dorms, a big dining room area, a meeting area, a movie theater, volleyball courts and basketball courts outside where the workers came for a designated free vacation for a few weeks. Of course, everything was free and the activities were organized. This was a feature of the Soviet Union building an egalitarian Socialist-Marxist society. And it wasn't posh. It was like a small standard state university built in the 1950's here in the USA. We stayed in the dorms. I had my own room. We shared a bathroom. It reminded me of my freshmen dorm at Northwestern. It was our base of operations. We took a bus into town every day to study Russian. Our woman teacher pushed us and was strict, calling on me when I lost focus. And then in a lot of the afternoons, we went into Leningrad and roamed around. It was just a fantastic experience. I remember once going by a shuttered church,

but there were all kinds of flowers put down outside so the people still worshipped. They just weren't allowed to practice it in public. An interesting thing was that there was a small building, like a hut, there on the resort campus. In it there was a bar. It was very simple. It was not exciting. There was a jukebox with some American tunes. And Tom Jones was on it. It was played over and over again. It was their favorite artist. The bar had simply a minimal amount of alcohol of different sorts, mostly vodka. I don't recall there being any ice. It was very plain. There were some tables scattered around. We spent time in there talking. We met some of the other foreigners, most were from Finland. And none of the Russian vacationers were allowed in there strangely enough. So it was just for foreigners, which I thought was kind of interesting. Candidly, Russia was a drab but stable society. No commercial advertising, neon signs, fast food restaurants, no traffic, and few cars, all small black ones. Clothing was not fashionable either. But I liked the country. And very little crime.

As far as training was concerned, I diligently trained, if not every day, close to it. And at this phase of the trip, the first two weeks, I did my running out around this Workers Resort, which was along the Gulf of Finland, this beautiful ancient looking beach with pebbles instead of sand, the sun still glowing some at the northern horizon at 1:00 a.m. I remember some nights, I would run up and down that beach into that setting sun at 10:00, 11:00, 12:00 at night. The sun glowed over the horizon almost all night. And I would just tear down that rocky beach, run as hard as I could. How far did I run? Oh, I don't know. I probably ran a mile in one direction fairly fast, pushing it, and caught my breath for a minute or two, and ran back. And down there were fishing homes, like cottages, right on the beach. These homes were made of wood with porches carved with designs and flowers. It was going back in time. The fishing boats were pulled up on the beach, made of wood, with a sail, and had the sailing masts sticking out of the middle of the boat. They were maybe 30 feet long and 8, 10 feet wide at the most. Just going back in time. But it was just a marvelous feeling. Not many Americans experience that. Far from the modern crowded life in the USA. You know my ethnic descent is from northern Europe along the Baltic Sea. I am a forest Baltic person deep inside. I actually feel comfortable in this environment with mall pine and white birch trees and extensive marshes, and the slight chilly breeze of the sea. A little bit austere and serious, like many of the ethnic people who live there, the Baltics, Germanic Prussian, Finnish, Russian, Polish.

I had another running route. We were along the coast and there were sand dunes and intermittent forests and some meadows. So I'd rundown a road and then cut off it into these sand dunes areas, where I would do hard striding over flat stretches and then sprinting up and down these sand hills. And lo and behold, the World War II relics were there for what I believe was the Finnish-Russian War of 1939 and the WW II siege of Leningrad by combined German- Finnish forces. This was about the perimeter front line. And at the top of these hills were pill boxes, which were these round, concrete fortifications with slits in them for guns to come out, and not just rifles, for artillery. And there was wire, old barbed wire spread around here and there that was used to stop the opposing forces from advancing. It was really a trip back in history and quite fascinating. I still am fascinated. It's a lot more than reading about it in history books. I relived it. Lucky me.

RUSSIAN PARTISANS WWII

NEVA RIVER LENINGRAD

The wide Neva River is beautiful in Leningrad, some of the Russian warships were parked there and submarines. It was just a beautiful setting. And I really was interested in, what we called, our enemy, because to me I didn't have any enemies And now our US Congress is saying that again, hmmmm... I am disheartened that our Congress and the mass media are calling Russia our enemy. This is dangerous and not really true. The Russians want reproachment with the USA. The cyber hacking is a defense tactic, although that does not justify it. Portraying Russia as an enemy is a political construct by our government and what is now called the Deep State and the Neocon attitude. The Deep State is not a group of people, but an IDEA or Attitude that floats around like a vapor, influencing various powerful people and the media. This US Deep State attitude is not happy with a centralized managed autocratic Russian "democracy", a powerful Russia (President Putin's words). Those people under the Deep State Spell want a western style democracy that is not a rival to US power and worldwide influence. Russia is very concerned about this attitude and considers it an existential threat to their country. Being an autocracy and monarchy for 800 years, the transition to a western democracy will take time to evolve. And Russia is the biggest country in the world with 11 time zones. Without centralization, it would be very difficult to control and manage their country. The Neocon Deep State follows an aggressive US foreign policy that will willingly use military power selectively and exert influence over governments

that do not conform to US strategic interests. Today they are also called Hawks. This is composed of many of the experts you see on news shows, former CIA officers and directors, generals, intellectuals, news experts, politicians including many in office now, and US officials. They believe the USA is the only exceptional country protecting the world from the bad guys, the evil leaders. With the exception of the madness in North Korea, I don't see any real country enemies. The USA has sponsored many autocratic tyrannical leaders when it is to their advantage. The Shah of Iran, President Pinochet of Chile who replaced an elected President Allende from 1973-1990, a Marxist, who did many constructive things for Chile, and guess who, Sadam Hussein of Iraq, a real tyrant, but who attacked Iran in a 7-year war 1979-1987. But Iraq was mostly a secular state friendly to Europe and the USA, a stable outpost for USA policy and a real buffer against Iran who was reasserting itself as a mid-east power after the 1979 revolution that overthrew the Shah of Iran, another dictator, and an ally of the US. Learning all this history has caused me some disillusion, but I still think the US is a great country but has been gradually losing its way. Watch Oliver Stones' long documentary, *The Untold Story of the USA*. My ideas were not gained from this all-encompassing movie, but coincidental and formulated over a long time of reading, studying, and thinking. Oliver Stone, a great director, produced *Platoon,* an anti-war movie about Vietnam staring Charlie Sheen in 1978, my favorite movie. Very realistic war movie depicts its horror. And us baby boomers know here again the US backed a ruthless corrupt dictator in South Vietnam. North Vietnam was defending their freedom after being dominated by the French since WW II until 1954 and then a series of USA South Vietnam puppet governments. What a terrible waste for all of Vietnam and the US soldiers (58,000 killed). North Vietnam lost 2-3 million civilians and soldiers. I have a high school friend, a basketball team athlete, who joined the Marines as a patriotic citizen and was killed there after 2 months. It is the law of unintended consequences causing great harm. And Oliver Stone invite me out to California. Anyone care to join me? By the way you don't have to accept what I say, find the truth and your opinion your own way. By writing this section I know some people might feel upset. But I am 70 and have early stage bladder cancer (it's ok now). I need to speak my mind. You younger people and leaders, God bless you, try to be rational and assess all the facts from all viewpoints before making a judgement, an opinion. I have great faith in the independently minded Millennium Generation, ages 18-35 in both the USA and Russia. And watch Oliver Stone's recent 4 hour interview of Vladimir Putin (on Showtime). President Putin appears very relaxed and candid with a sense of humor. Oliver has a kind questioning respectful demeanor, maybe a touch naive. Putin is very shrewd and well informed and disciplined.

The USA feared the spread of the doctrine, Communism, that said capitalistic countries would cease to exist due to economic evolution, peacefully. The violence of the Soviet Stalinist period in the 1930's created fear in the minds of Americans (and Ukrainians). But also remember Russia was also afraid of the West and America. Germany had just destroyed the country in two World Wars. WW II had ended 23 years ago in 1968 when I was there. The Cold War was on. The USA had many nuclear weapons on B52 attack bombers just outside the Russian borders, a 1-hour flight to Moscow and minutes to Leningrad. A little scary if you ask me. Remember the movie, Dr. Strangelove?

Two aspects about Russian attitudes (and China which is similar) are that Russian has been an empire since 1250 and now it is ascending to that historical status. It also is a country that has no history of western liberal democracy. It has been run by Tsars or Kings and the Communist Party. It is and has been a highly centralized state controlling a vast country. Russia has also been invaded numerous times since 1850 by Europe resulting in devastation. This makes it defensive in nature and cautious. So there is no reason to expect Russia to become a passive liberal democracy. Actions that expand NATO, cancel arms treaties, and call it a US enemy only serve to increase Russian concerns about outside aggression to weaken their homeland.

I discuss this in depth in my new upcoming book about the political and military conflict between the USA, Russia, Ukraine, and China. I believe it is my duty to express the Russian and Chinese viewpoint. <u>Candidly, it is being a US patriot to express a minority controversial perspective and risk criticism.</u>

Let me tell you about the Aeroflot Russian passenger jets! Yes, the Russians were prepared militarily if invaded again. They were twin jet engines, what I would call "nimble and sporty". And the nosecone under the cockpit was transparent, a bomb site! These aircraft could be converted quickly to bombers if needed! Inside they were Spartan-plain canvas seats without foam padding, they looked like a military transport, and felt like it.

We took busses into the rural areas. There were these beautiful little homes made of wood. They were one story cottages, called Dachas, with flowers and gardens all around them, very quaint with the typical, old European woman, standing outside smiling. One time a part of our group took a bus on a Sunday about a 30-minute ride to the Finnish border and got out and wandered around this small town, taking pictures. And a man came up and said, "Come with us. I want to take you and show you the library and museum." And when they got to this building, lo and behold, the library was the local center for the Communist Party headquarters in that town. They were interviewed for several hours and their

film was taken because right there was a ballistic missile base along the Finnish border, a defense fortification or offense, depending upon your point of view.

So I went to Moscow for three weeks. And my memory is a little vague. But I remember jogging to a nearby park, joining a man my age playing basketball. He was studying to be a diplomat. And of course, this is 1968, the height of the Vietnam War. He wanted to go to Vietnam to be a Russian diplomat in Hanoi. I thought that so fascinating. Here we are, I'm right up with somebody face to face, the opposing side, playing basketball with me. How ironic is that. But to me, there was no opposing side, as I have said. I sometimes wonder what happened to him. And I ran around this park. It was a combination of short, hard distance runs (2 miles or so) and fast smooth striding with short rest periods. But they were very intense. I wasn't just fooling around. I was training. We had a marvelous time in Moscow. One of the most interesting, fascinating places to visit is Red Square alongside the Kremlin. The Russian Government has the Victory Day Parade there every May 9th, the day Germany surrendered in WW II. This is a televised event on U Tube. Watch it. (GOOGLE Red Square 2018 Victory Day Parade English). You will see soldiers marching, weapons on parade, and President Putin making a 10-minute speech. The commentary is like CNN in English. Very clear. This event honors the Russian people lost during WW II and the defeat of German fascism. Russia lost 20 million civilians and 8 million soldiers. They gradually pushed Germany back from the edge of Moscow to Berlin from January 1942-April 1945. This broke the back of the German military. Alongside this beautiful square is St. Basil's Cathedral, the magnificent Russian Orthodox Church with the onion spires you have seen, multiple colored, and watching over the Kremlin. It was first built in 1331, a long long time ago. What I felt there in Red Square and still do when I see videos of it today, is a really a deep sense of the Russian soul, a deep sense of Russian history. Two Russian WWII songs you must listen to on UTUBE are *"Katusha"* and *"Farewell to Slavyanka"* This will give you a deeper sense of Russian traditional beautiful hopeful songs from the heart. You know Moscow began in 1250 and Kremlin means fortress. For 200 years the Mongol Empire conquered and controlled Russia, from 1250-1450. But they let Russia have a degree of self-governing. After 1450 the Russian Empire expanded and contracted, waxed and waned. You can seem to feel a sense of history. There is just this tremendous sense of power. I know the Russians have a very strong connection to Mother Earth and Mother Russia, which goes to their heart and soul, and is not nearly as obvious in the USA and Canada from what I can tell. It is an emotional historical connection. You can feel it there*, you can sense this civilization is to be respected and politically a force to be reckoned with and handled fairly with equity.*

To get a glimpse of Russia today on a casual warm afternoon in Gorki Park on Victory Day after the Parade GOOGLE: "Real Russia" Gorki Park episode 47. It is very humorous. There are 146 episodes of Real Russia that show a glimpse into Russian life today. Very interesting and not political. I recently spoke long distance to the film maker Sergei Baklykov.

Russian lady distance runner in the forest. Russians like their forests 2015

Contemporary Russian woman 2017

While we are on this history lesson did you know Lithuania and Sweden occupied Russia and came up right to Moscow in 1610. In 1708 Sweden and Poland attacked Russia again and came within 10 miles of Moscow before being pushed back at the Battle of Poltava. It's significant that several Empires came so close to Moscow but had to retreat. (Napoleon/France, Germany, Sweden.). In 1650 Ukraine was

split in half by Poland and Russian opposing forces. Conflict and outside control there is not new. Far western Ukraine was once part of Poland and also Austro-Hungary and sided with Germany when the Germany Army invaded Ukraine on its way to Russia. Borders change. The ancient Rus people originated in an area comprising parts of today's Russia, Ukraine, and Belarus (White Russia). Families today from all three countries are intermingled and the languages are almost identical as is their Russian Orthodox Christian religion. That area is centered on the ancient and current cities of Novgorod and Vladimir and has strong historical connections to Kiev. See, it's not so simple. And do you know that during a lengthy religious service lasting 2-3 hours all people stand. There are no pews, seats, benches! A Russian told me this to show respect to Christ and the saints.

Shut Orthodox Church with flowers in front

I hope to go back there soon to visit for a few weeks and meet some friends I've met on the Internet, Russian businessmen, some professors and economists, maybe a government official or two and some Communist Party members and KGB agents from the 1970's. I hope to teach a survey course in economics there and do some lectures on USA economic issues. I study Russian now. It's one of my sidelights, Russian politics, history and the language. Who knows maybe I can give the Russian middle-distance runners and coaches some good advice based on this book. That would be good for all of us. I almost ran in a track meet in Leningrad in 1968. A Russian and Finnish local city club were competing. The 800 went in 1:50, won by a Finn. I might have won. This would have caused a big political problem for the Russian coach.

Let me tell you that it was a marvelous trip. But the interesting part from the training standpoint, which I'm sure you're all interested in, is I still trained hard. That was six weeks, really, of very intensive training, no interval work, no spiked track shoes, all in flats, running with a sense of inspiration, and with a tremendous amount of really, basically intensive fartlek is what I would call it. Around parks, on beaches, sand hills, meadows and farms. And to tell you the truth, it kept me in great shape. I was concerned about my conditioning. It just goes to show you, that you don't need to be running hard intervals on a track for most of a season to develop racing condition.

Some other key points about the trip I need to mention. Many people inquired if the USA was so great how come your leaders were assassinated, Martin Luther King, Robert Kennedy, and President John Kennedy. I had no answer. The Russian people said the American people were great, but the problem was your government. They still do. Wandering around Moscow one day about eight of us came across a small storefront with a big map of Vietnam taped to the window. And wow, it was the National Liberation Front or Viet Cong Embassy (those South Vietnamese fighting against the South Vietnam government). We were invited in for tea and chocolates and seated at a long table. Their representative gave a gentle candid talk about their point of view and said he was sorry some of us might fight there and be killed. It shook me up, but I was amazed to be having this diplomatic experience while a war was raging half way around the world. We went to a ballet inside a theater in the Kremlin. In the audience were many Chinese high-ranking officials in those high neck stiff khaki uniforms with red epaulets. It was very strange to be in a roomful of people who also were considered enemies, anti-capitalist revolutionary states. And astounding to be with them right there in such a cultural peaceful place. Also the stores did not have cash registers, but used an abacus to calculate purchases, you know these round wooden balls on wires on a piece of wood. Several times young Russians asked to buy the blue jeans I was wearing for a high price and send them cassettes with The Beatles and other rock music. This was all illegal with stiff penalties. Ouch. The meat shop I went into had almost no meat. I remember a few large whole fish for sale. Consumer goods were shoddy. Shipments from Austria and Hungary had long waiting lines in the streets to purchase shoes. Appears free markets do work. President Putin said about 2012, "Russians who don't think back fondly about the Soviet Union have no heart. Those who want to return to it have no head." So true! Today Russia has a capitalistic free market economy somewhat controlled (managed) by a strong government. Hmmm...well maybe today the USA has a few somewhat similar characteristics. Corporations, big money, trying to do what is best for America, and themselves, exerting strong influence. What do you think? Consumer goods and everyday culture are the same as in Europe and the USA. We went into Lenin's tomb alongside the Kremlin wall. A very long line of

Russians waited outside. Naturally we didn't have to wait. Unbelievable, I actually stood along the real preserved body of Lenin under a glass casket, 2 feet away. As Americans casually do, I slouched and put a hand into my pocket. A soldier standing behind me uttered a loud command and pulled my arm out of my pocket and snapped it down! I was very disrespectful. Just goes to show you. Other things, absolutely no commercial advertising, but giant signs on buildings declaring loyalty to Marxist Russia, Lenin, and Soviet Workers and Soviet power. Also no world news except limited interpretations filtered by the Communist party. When one of us brought back a Time magazine from the American Embassy we all read it cover to cover. There really was a news blackout. No visible restaurants and fast food franchises. Hardly any cars, but overstuffed busses, people squeezing in for a place to stand, all wore the same drab trenchcoats. At the hotels an older lady was in the lobby checking on you. You gave her your key, a big key hanging from a large wooden ball. Couldn't lose that. Statues of Lenin were everywhere. But the art in the old monasteries was dramatic, deeply meaningful on a flat surface and called an icon. We went to Zagorsk, an ancient monastery. Part of our group went on a quick weekend trip to Kiev, Ukraine. Get the connection everyone? Not a simple situation today.

-

LENIN'S TOMB Red Square--Founder of Soviet Communism

But do I remember the delicious Russian ice cream sold by women street vendors from their carts! Each piece was slightly different, seemingly hand made. You would love it! There were also soda machines

on the streets. With a weak fruit tasting fizzy water. You put in a few kopecks and pressed a button and your favorite flavor flowed out---into a plastic glass that was put back after drinking and reused by everyone! But it did have a rinse nozzle with no soap.

The schools. Then and I believe now, the students were very serious and disciplined. When a teacher entered the room, the students stood up. Yes, for real! English was taught to everybody starting in Grade 1. The teachers made you work. I studied Russian in a classroom for a month. I remember. No nonsense. Today high school in Russia is more rigorous than in the USA. To graduate you must pass a difficult exam. Ordinarily this takes up to a year of extra study and several attempts. So most students graduate in 5 years. Some exams are oral 1 on 1 student to professor. Ahead of time the student might be given 3 questions to study and not know which will be used for the exam until it begins. For higher education students are put into the "ACADEMIC" so called college bound track (about 1/3) and others into the Vocational track (2/3). Today many Russians attended vocational school and have productive jobs, important to building a socialist Soviet society then and now a free market economy. Many people were granted their own modest apartments (by Western standards) after the demise of the Soviet Union in 1992 and still own them today. They were owned by the State during the Soviet era. They pay only for utilities. These 2-bedroom apartments are about 500-600 square feet and a 1 bedroom 300-400 square foot, ½ the size of US apartments. But they are comfortable, but look tired, a little run down. Outside they all are a boring similarity, as Soviet authorities tried to create an egalitarian socialist state in the past.

I have a Ukrainian-Russian student from Donbass, the conflict area. He is very disciplined intellectually, age 20, and in the US Air Force. Arrived here at age 13. He said senior math in his American High School was the same as he had in 7th grade in Ukraine. The US has dropped to #38 in math internationally. Russia is about 20th, behind the Scandinavian and Asian schools. The US is 24th in science for age 16. Do you think education is critical for the future standard of living? I recently went to a Russian picnic here and met two professors of mathematics and a physics professor. All middle aged and schooled in Russia and now teaching at University of New Mexico. I am impressed.

My Russian Language Teacher 1968 Right: Today old Moscow Soviet apartments

Boys near Finnish Gulf --Viet Cong or National Liberation Front Embassy map of Vietnam conflict 1968

Well, the trip to Russia began to end, and we flew to Vilnius, which is the capital and ancient city of Lithuania. A wonderful place. Here we met a stranger who attached himself to us, why I don't know. He had blond hair and German father. Probably a German WWII soldier. Whose surprised? He drove an expensive large motorcycle, very unusual in those days. Our group used to talk about politics at night and he would say, hush, quiet, they might be listening. Strangely, he sent me a letter to my home in the USA some time later with a picture. A few years later in 1970 I was undergoing a top secret security clearance for an army intelligence post. And guess what. The Defense Intelligence Agency knew about this and asked me a few questions! Still amazes me. Some might say I and some of the students were being sized up as possible Russian future sources. Russia has always had a very effective intelligence service. What if I or another student had a long career in the US Foreign Service State Department and

maintained an open mind to Russian ideas?

Then we took a train, a Russian train. It was a steam locomotive with a giant red star in front for the Soviet Union, just like you saw in *Dr.Zhivago*, the movie. IMPRESSIVE!! And it was just marvelous going on this train across Europe. We stayed in a compartment for 6 people facing one another. Outside was a passageway alongside the train windows which were often open. No air conditioning. The interesting point is that when we got to the Polish border, which was in a bucolic beautiful meadow, there was a trestle overhead, and there were actually armed soldiers marching back and forth. And it really surprised me that these two countries, which were part of the Warsaw Pact, joined together, would have such an autocratic, highly threatening border patrol. We spent an hour there while the train was investigated. We also had to show our passports.

Glory to the Soviet Teacher (translation) 1968

SOVIET WOMAN 1980

I couldn't understand why that would be. But it shows you something on the strictness and the tightly wound Soviet system. It wasn't all that friendly. But looking out, maybe a quarter mile out there was an old small church with a spire. And believe it or not, a woman dressed like, what I would call, folk dress, with a babushka over her head, was on a hay wagon being pulled by some horses on a dirt road in a meadow. I couldn't believe it in that day and age that is how agriculture was being done, a hay wagon pulled by horses. I also visited a Russian collective farm which was very modern, clean, and tidy with a large staff of workers trained by the Russian state to farm. They had new tractors and modern mechanized farm implements. But agricultural output could not keep up with the USA. This year, 2019, Russia has become the #1 wheat exporter in the world.

We stayed in Warsaw 2 days. It had more luxury goods and appeared better off than Russia. The Soviets had built a large spiraled pointed skyscraper office building in the city center, what the Poles called their gift from Russia. The Poles were not happy being controlled by the Soviet Union. But the Food!! What a difference and improvement from Russia. In Russia most of the meat was non-descript plain fried cutlets of some sort. We called it mystery meat. The vegetables were peas, carrots, cabbage, pickled beets often mixed into a salad with a sour cream like dressing and boiled potatoes. It tasted good but the meals were monotonous. And all were served with Black Rye bread. But the beet soup, Borscht, was delicious! But when we arrived in Warsaw, we were treated to a feast identical to the wedding banquets I had been to as a child in Chicago. Steaming plates of ham, beef, polish sausage, mashed potatoes, gravy, carrots, cabbage, and breads and rolls. Wow!

We moved on. We pulled into the East Berlin station where the train line ended. I remember I saw some Russian soldiers out the window, and I shouted how are you soldiers in Russian and one of the soldiers turned and looked at me and shouted back. Then we spent some time in East Berlin, which was totally bombed out. It still looked like it hadn't been rebuilt since World War II. Empty areas all over. No new buildings. Whereas West Berlin was a bustling beautiful commercial city full of people with handsome clothes. And there was a giant Coca Cola sign as we moved from East to West Berlin through the Vandenberg Gate. It was just totally amazing. I actually liked the buzz and the excitement of this giant neon sign after having none of this for 5 weeks in the Soviet Union. The other amazing thing there was our visit to the Olympic Stadium where the Olympics were held in 1936 during the Nazi/Hitler era of Germany. I just remember it as being an immense stadium. It had a sense of grandeur and power to it, which is representative of German culture. Just awesome. Here is where Jesse Owens of the USA, an African-American black man, won his gold medals. And remember he interviewed me when I was in high school. So ironic. I just wanted to run a lap around the track.

Well, we moved on and went to England. And the running part I remember there is that I stayed for a couple days on a farm. And what I did is I ran around the edges along the fence on a slightly lumpy pasture grassy ground. There were cows grazing in the middle. I ran fast 440s in flats, really intense speedplay, pushed it. I guess it was about a 440, thereabouts. Real intensive fartlek or workouts a few times. The area was near Tunbridge Wells, a beautiful quaint area of narrow roads with stone walls alongside, and village inns. Nothing quite like this in the USA.

Ollan Cassell, world record US 400m Olympian in 1964 became Director of the US NAAU and organized numerous track & field meets between the USA and Russia/Soviet Union from 1966 to 1988. This lessened Cold War tension and provided spirited friendly competition between the two great powers of the world which was good for mutual understanding and peaceful coexistence. He has a book just published about this period and the US Olympic program

Echo Lake Olympic Training Camp Site at 7300 feet near South Lake Tahoe California. Note track built carefully in a forest to preserve trees. 1968

LAKE TAHOE

Well, the summer was coming to an end, and so I flew back to Chicago. I literally spent a day there and hopped on a plane, with my paid ticket from the Olympic Committee, to Reno, Nevada and then took I a bus up to the South Lake Tahoe training facility, which was about 20 miles up at Echo Lake at 7,000-foot altitude just south of South Lake Tahoe, a beautiful area. Since the Olympics were in Mexico City, at 7300-foot elevation, the Olympic Committee built this training facility. The airline lost my luggage which was a bad omen of things to come. We were housed in trailers. I had a roommate. But I tried to cram in too much running in three weeks to get ready for the try-outs.

In the mornings, Mark Winzenreid and I jogged on a trail through some rocky area, through a forest near Echo Lake. And then I did interval work on the track in the afternoon. It's hard to remember it all exactly. But one thing stands out is that four days before the Olympic try-outs, my coach Bob Ehrhart showed up. And I guess I wanted to tune up with some 400s, but I was a little too pumped and I ran them both in 48 and a 49 with about a five-minute rest in between, which is really fast for me, about the fastest I had ever done. Four days later, I think I was still tight from that, and I ran a real lousy prelim about 1:51+ and finished way in the back. I just didn't have it. Then I went back home to Chicago. But

then two days later, I came down with mononucleosis, a very serious strep sore throat. Maybe I was getting weakened, that I did too much all summer. And by the time the try-outs came in early September, I was really finished, getting stale.

It was quite a nice time though being with all those athletes, eating in the mess hall they had built up there. They had built a training camp and the track. There's really a beautiful forest. They have trees running alongside the track. Some of you will remember that very well. I remember that was where I saw, we went down to South Lake Tahoe, a bunch of us in some cars and saw the movie *The Graduate* in a drive-in. So every time I see that Dustin Hoffman movie, I remember this time very well. I was also becoming the uncertain graduate soon.

I came back to Oak Lawn in the Chicago area, and recuperated from this trip. I lost about seven pounds. I should've run that way because I looked a lot thinner, just a small decrease in weight. But I ran a good Fall cross-country season. It was my Senior year. But I was inconsistent. I did the hard training I've discussed about, which is what you really need to do for three months. And I remember the Big Ten Meet was at Ohio State in early November. It was one these warm, kind of humid weekends. It was run at the Ohio State University Golf Course near the Olentangy River. Our track manager, Rich Christopher, and I – (Rich is still my friend years later –we have breakfast twice a year). We were both considering law school. I had all kinds of ideas of where to go to law school. So the day before the meet on a Friday afternoon, we walked all over that Ohio State campus. It tired me out. I had done it again like two years before at The University of Wisconsin Indoor Big Ten Meet. We both went into the law school. We were looking around there in the library. We met with one of the deans and talked to him for a little while. Then he kicked us out. He didn't want non-law students just walking around there looking at the facilities and being curiosity seekers.

Well, the next day was a nice day to run, warm, calm, cloudy. And I died. Out of the 70 runners I was probably 63th. The three of us Northwestern guys Bob Hinshaw, Rich Boudreaux (Rich became station chief for the Wall Street Journal newspaper in Spain) and me were all together there in the last seven places. Quite humiliating. I just couldn't even move the last mile and a half. I just jogged it in stiff as a board. Rich is from Shreveport, Louisiana so we kiddingly nicknamed him "the Ragin Cajun ".

Well, needless to say, I had from July into December in 1968, that's five good months -- July, August, September, October, November -- of base work, cross country running, hard fartlek, and a little bit of track work in the middle just to tune myself up. From the middle of November until mid- December (5 weeks) when we went home from Northwestern after our quarterly finals, I did the same thing as the year before but more intensively. Once or twice a week I ran 20 x 220 on the indoor track around 30 seconds with about a 100 jog or about a minute. And the last 220 I'd crank it up and cruise it in the 27-28 range. In the middle, there was a basketball court, and the varsity basketball team was practicing getting ready for their big season. I was the only track guy there running by myself because the cross-country season had ended, and I was the only person with enough ambition and dedication to run an off season one-month workout regimen. I also ran outdoors, what I would call, my three to four mile hard runs or fartlek, i.e. speed play, through the northern suburbs and out west of the university and back through these beautiful Wilmette and Evanston neighborhoods that were so stately and calming.

In mid-December, I went home and did a little running in the forest preserves, but then I would go down to The University of Chicago a few times and did some, what I would call, light speed work just to tune up a little, like eight 220s in the high 20s or maybe a couple of 440s in the mid-50s. But I did run in the annual Holiday Meet, which they still run in honor of Ted Haydon and is put on by The University of Chicago Track Club, UCTC it's called. And I'm not sure exactly what I ran, but probably a 2:12 1000 Yard Run, which wasn't bad, and probably finished first. Then in January I went back to school. The first week at Northwestern that began that marvelous indoor season where I was at my peak conditioning of my life.

To summarize: I had run five months of hard modified distance work, speed play fartlek, some track workouts in September and mid-November to December 30th, and a hard cross country season where again our fundamental workouts were 20 x 440 or 4 x 1 mile or a hard accelerating six-mile run. Those seemed to be the three key ones. And a five-mile (8000m) race every weekend for about seven weeks in a row.

December was the transitional month. As I have said, from mid-December for about three weeks to early January, I ran some outdoor fartlek and four-mile distance runs in the kind of get myself tuned up for the indoor season at Northwestern University. The McGaw Hall fieldhouse indoor dirt track with some sand sprinkled on top was very good for training, not so great for racing. But I still ran good race times there.

McGaw Hall Basketball and Track Fieldhouse 1968

UNIVERSITY OF ILLINOIS INDOOR BIG 10 MEET 1969

THE SEASON-WORLD RECORD-MY LIFETIME PEAK CONDITION--- January to March 1969

Finish of Preliminary 1000 in 2.10 at Big Ten Meet 1969 night before world record. It felt easy.

I already explained how I trained during this period to get prepared for that World Record 1000 Yard Run (January-March 1969). It amazes me what I ran in a period of about 10 weeks. In workouts, I ran a 1:50.5 880 (149.7 800 meter) which broke the school indoor record unofficially. I ran a 2:09 1000-yard run in practice by myself which was a tremendous Big Ten race time (I had set the Big Ten record the year before in 2:09). I ran several races in the low 1:50s, 1:51 at the Mason Dixon Games. And then I ran the 2:06 1,000 Yard Run at the Big Ten Meet and the following week finished fourth at the NCAA meet at Detroit's Cobo Arena in 2:09 on the wooden board tracks they used to have. I was in great shape. I ran a couple of indoor miles in 4:08 and 4:09 and finished second to Jim Ryun at Michigan State Relays. I think I could have eventually run 3:59 if I had focused on the mile. Really, I mean it. And overall, I was in terrific shape. I was running mile relay anchors around 49 after having already run two races. (Best 440 split was 47 flat at te Big Ten Meet). I also ran a mile and a half indoors by myself in 6:42, which is a very fast pace for a half-miler. That is equivalent of about a 4:26 mile split. So I could run anything from about a 48 second 440 yard relay split, all the way up to probably near a 9:00 minute two mile if I concentrated on that event. I was in the ZONE, in terrific shape!

From 1967-71 I ran twenty-five 880 yard/800 meter races from 1:50-1:47 and six 1000 yard run races under 2:10. I was first in major races and relays 9 times including 2 world records.

I remember in January, we ran some meets at The University of Chicago and down at the University of Illinois as my conditioning progressed. I ran a mile finally in 4:07.9 at the Western Michigan Relays. I went out in front, took the lead, and ran even pace all the way. The following week, I went up to Michigan State Relays and ran the mile that year. My opponent was Jim Ryun, the Olympian. I was very pumped up hoping to run about a 4:06. I ran a 4:09.4. I ran an even pace. I led the whole race. I probably ran about a 30 on the last 200. But Ryun ran about a 25 or 26, went by me like I was standing still, as if he was running a practice 220 all out. He ran about a 4:05.7 as I remember. I was trying to see how fast I could run the mile. There was a little part of me that wanted to see if I could move up to the mile. Plus, I had decided that type of training is something that made sense to me. And maybe some of it was inadvertent. But I actually trained more for the mile and ran the 1000 Yard Run, and that's what led me to success I believe. As I said, a 1:48 800 is an interval workout of four (4) times 27 seconds with a zero second interval. Something to remember.

The season went on through February, we ran some meets here and there. I ran a 1:51 at the Mason Dixon indoor meet in Louisville Kentucky on the 220-yard indoor board track and won, that was exciting. We competed in some smaller meets locally, but one against the University of Minnesota at the end of February I remember well. I ran 4:14 for the mile-won. Then a 1:55 880 after that race. I followed the Minnesota runner and ran 30, 30, 30 and then 25 in the last 220, just smoked everyone, and then a 49 split on the mile relay. And this was all at McGaw Hall. This was a Friday meet, I believe, and that left me seven workout days until the Big Ten preliminary 1000. I thought I had an extra day in there to train. So on Saturday early evening at 6 PM, it's dark out. I put on my sweats, went across the street and ran sprints back and forth on a cobblestone, old style Evanston street in a residential area next to Marywood Academy with those old-fashioned street lamps. I would guess this distance was about 120 yards. I sprinted hard back and forth for a total of 10 times or 20 sprints. Literally, the only rest was I'd stop and turn around and sprint back. I was trying to squeeze in one last workout that would give me staying power at the end of the race. That workout, I believe, really helped in that record 1,000. It just tuned me up enough to have that very strong finish. But it was a little risky and could have injured me.

Well, Sunday, unfortunately, I was stiff as a board. And as I recall, I didn't run at all. Monday, I went into practice. In retrospect, I don't know why I ran so hard on Saturday just a week before the BIG TEN Meet. But I was tight so I just ran six 220's around 30, and my legs were dead. I called it quits for the day. But actually that was good because that was the equivalent of a good warm-up, which flushed out my legs and got the lactic acid out. The next day on Tuesday, I said to myself, let's tune up for the meet. Pace work. I felt really good, and I ran three 440s in 56, 54 and 58 with a 440 jog in between, which was probably a little over two minutes. And it was very smooth. I ran the first one easy, then I decided to pick it up to 54, which is little faster than race pace. And then I said I'll run one more and really ease off, and I ran a 58. And that was my tuning workout. And that's what I recommend for you 800-meter runners, to run a similar workout before a major race. Wednesday, I did my traditional 7, 6, 5 minute run workout. Thursday, we went down to Illinois, and I was very excited. I did an indoor warm-up and worked up a good sweat. And then Friday night I ran the preliminary in the 1000 yards. Roger Merchant was behind me, my friend from Michigan State. And I just cruised it. I ran about a 2:10. It was so easy. I never had to pick it up at the end. When the race ended, I was breathing pretty hard but I never got tired, so I knew something big was coming up.

Well, the next day was the Big Ten 1,000. The night before on Thursday the coaches had their meeting and released who they would have run in each event. Unfortunately, Mark Winzenreid and Ron Kuchinski, my two major rivals and two of the best middle-distance runners in the United States, went into the 1,000 yard run. Why one of them could not have run the 880 is beyond me, or even both of them. So I was extremely nervous, and I was the Big Ten defending champ. This was my last indoor college race, and I did not want to finish less than first. I remember that morning. I ate a good breakfast about 8:00 AM. Pancakes and eggs, lots of energy food. The race was about 2:00 PM. And Bob Ehrhart, my coach, found right by my feet as we closed the motel door a one-dollar bill, which he inscribed to me for good luck, and I still have that one dollar bill in my scrapbook, believe it or not. Bob has passed away from cancer about 10 years ago. He became the coach of Drake University and Director of the Drake Relays and was well known and respected throughout United States track and field athletics.

So we got to the meet. I was nervous, folks. We went up to the starting line, and my legs felt like concrete. I said, "Oh, my god. I'm going to have a bad race." Well, we took off and the feeling immediately left me. But I decided I would have to run a steady conservative pace, which I did. I would guess I was 55 seconds at the 440 point. But I was so far behind Ron Kuchinski and Mark Winzenreid, they looked like they were half a lap ahead of me. In reality, they were probably 20 to 30 yards or about a good 2 to 3 seconds. I just couldn't run at that fast of a start and have a good finish because again I was a strength endurance runner. Those guys had a little more speed, but also the ability to run a hard race by going out fast. Consequently, I was also playing it very conservatively, especially since my legs felt heavy at the beginning. But I felt good, bouncy, and smooth during the race. Roger Merchant of Michigan State was right ahead of me too so I was running fourth. Then with about one and third laps to go on the oversized Illinois track (that would probably be about 350 yards left to run, the track is 267 yards), I took off. I went by Roger. I went down the straightaway, the 70 yard straightaway and went by Kuchinski like he was standing still. At the beginning of the second to last turn, I came around the curve, looked up and I saw Mark Winzenreid. He must have been a good 15 yards ahead of me. And I thought, "This is it. Do or Die." And I sprinted all out. And within 70 yards on the straightaway, I caught him and passed him quickly at the 880 mark at 1:50.5. And I sprinted in and as I came around the turn, looking ahead with 60 yards to go, and I saw daylight and I said, "I'm going to win. I'm going to win. I'm going to win!" And I just sprinted in with all I had and won the race. Mark Winzenreid was only six-tenths of a second behind me at 2:06.6. Ron Kuchinski, 2:07.8, and Roger Merchant about 2:09. I ran a 2:06 flat, which tied Peter Snell's world record and set a new Big Ten record by three seconds of which

I'd run the year before in 2:09.1. (2:09, 2:10 were the typical 1,000 Yard Times most Big Ten runners were running in those days who were the leading runners in the conference before 1968). Was I excited! And relieved! Larry Wieczorek, the prior year's Big Ten Mile Champ from Iowa, coaxed me into taking a victory lap. I jogged around and waved to the crowd. And afterwards, they were just flashing lights and cameras all over the place. I had my picture in the Sunday headlines of the *Chicago Tribune* sports page "Schultz Ties World Record," in big bold letters. I still have that. I have it encased and laminated it in plastic. *The Chicago Sun Times, Daily News, Chicago American*, all had great pictures and articles about me, and I looked like a million bucks. I looked so happy and so sublime. Ghee, I wish I could feel like that today. Then I ran the anchor leg 440 of the mile relay in 47.3 which was the best time I had ever run even though we were way behind because our other three relay runners weren't competitive.

Me receiving baton anchor leg mile relay at Northwestern McGaw Hall Indoor Meet 1969 one week prior to Big 10 Conference Meet at Illinois. Note the basketball bleachers and the narrow track. Exit out of tunnel on curve in background. Ran 49.0 after racing mile and 880.

FINISH 1000 YARD RUN WORLD RECORD 2:06 AND ON MEDAL PLATFORM AFTER RACE

Finish 1000 Yard Run World Record 2:06 THIS IS IT! THE BIG PAYOFF

Receiving 1ST Place Medal after Big 10 victory World Record.

Well, after that race, I got all kinds of accolades. An ABC TV sportscaster interviewed me for the evening Chicago News. That I liked. And even in the spring when I walked to class somehow people knew who I was, who I didn't have the faintest idea who they were. And they were all saying, "Nice going, Ralph. How are you, Ralph?" Strangely enough, probably like a lot of celebrities, I got tired of the attention and it really got irritating. Talk about an ego. On Sunday morning after the race, my fraternity, Delta Tau Delta, put a gigantic banner on our shelter fraternity house recognizing me. It was great, thanks Bros! And Fred Radewagen thank you for putting an article in the Delt Fraternity national magazine about my induction into the Northwestern University Hall of Fame in 2011. Fred is active in national politics and a Delt supporter. His politics are different than mine, but that's OK Fred. He lives in Washington DC with his wife, a Congressional Representative from the Pacific Islands, a United States

Territory. In college he was our social director who arranged our fraternity parties including a Toga party which I never forgot. Well, in March a week or two later when I went to the NCAAs, at Detroit's Cobo Arena, I finished fourth. I ran a 2:09.1. The winner was about 2:08. I just was a bigger sized guy. I couldn't run that well on the boards. But it was satisfying. Keith Colburn finished a step behind. He became my buddy and was from Harvard. The pleasure from winning was well earned and I deserved it. I had come a long way from running laps around the gym and high school sidewalk. I never dreamed in high school I would achieve such incredible success.

A funny anecdote is that the other two Northwestern track and field athletes that won Big 10 Championships in 1968-69 were non-athletic scholarship athletes, called "walk-ons". Rich Feezel won the 1969 Indoor Long Jump and Frank Cormia won the Outdoor Triple Jump in 1968. Rich was from southern Illinois whose father ran a large hog farm. Frank went on to medical school and of all things he recently is living just outside Albuquerque, NM in the Sandia Mountains. He has a very long prospectors beard and an eclectic personality. Congratulations guys.

The season ended at the end of March at the indoor Central AAU meet at The University of Chicago track. I think I ran the 1000 probably about 2:10, but I won the race. By then I was tiring out after 8 months of training and racing.

READERS NOTES: Do you agree with me that very little speedwork is necessary to run a good 800m?

TIRED AFTER RECORD RACE

Never in a lifetime would I have expected to run so fast and tie a world record. My goal was just to finish first. Years of training had worked including running in woods, hills, snow, streets. And always refusing to give up, but looking ahead, one step at a time. And long and short-term goals. Running, racing was serious business and no one, nothing, was going to stop me or get in my way.

With my Coach Bob Ehrhart prior to race offering encouragement. 1969

By my Junior year I created mostly my own workout schedule. Bob was a great pole vaulter at Northwestern in 1954 and Big 10 Champion. He also was a Marine. I wish our team could have shown him better performances. He was a dedicated coach and athlete.

READERS NOTES: How do your workouts compare to mine? Do you think my method would help you improve? Avoid injuries and illness? List your key workouts. Do you emphasize endurance pace intervals or intensive speed work? Running 20x400 every Monday from September 1 to November 15 builds great strength endurance. You increase aerobic lung capacity.

OUTDOORS 1969-Senior Year.

The season ended, and my roommate and track team photographer Bob Hinshaw and I drove to Florida to Fort Lauderdale for a spring trip. We stayed with his aunt. The sort of strange things people do. But after all I was a 21-year-old college student, I had a social life too. We spent a night in Daytona Beach, and it was evening with the full moon out. And we actually went out in the water up to our chest. It was a calm night. Well, you know, that's when the sharks are out in that depth of water. That area is known for having many dangerous sharks. How foolish was I? It was a beautiful evening. I would never do it again, and I'm sure nobody else would either. Lucky we weren't attacked during feeding time. Well, I spent several days in Fort Lauderdale. Bob and I had a typical good time. I did some easy running in a park, jogging and striding a couple of different times just to maintain some fitness. I got stung by a jellyfish on the beach. Ouch, it stung. But we poured some gasoline on it and the pain went away. And then we went back. Then almost another tragedy. In Kentucky, Bob lost control of our drive away car we were driving for an individual and went off the road and just missed a Corvette and hit a telephone pole. We weren't injured. But somehow miraculously, we took the car, had it towed into a shop. It was near Hopkinsville, Kentucky. And believe it or not, the car with just a few repairs was drivable. Amazing isn't it? Lucky, very lucky.

ABOVE: Running in Fort Lauderdale, Florida on vacation 1969 after World Record race

Everglades vista and boat ride. Note alligator

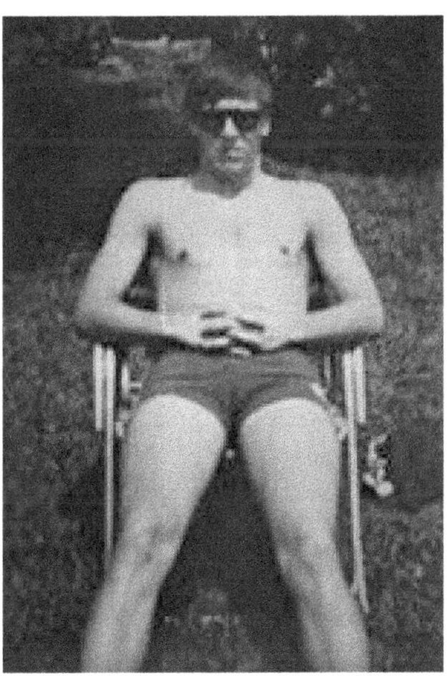

Fort Lauderdale Florida relaxing vacation March 1969

Well outdoor season started. And as I said the first week or two I did some endurance training outside and some intervals, 20 x 440 once or twice and some 3 to 5 mile hard fartlek runs and 3 x 1200m. (3/4 mile) slow on the track just to tune up in that lousy weather we had then. The track was a little mushy, a little soft, and it was cold and blustery a lot of those days.

We went to Missouri in early April, beautiful down there, a different climate. Spring had arrived there. I ran an 880 in 1:50.4, won the race. Then we went to the Ohio State Relays. I won the 880 there about 1:50.5 again and ran on a relay. An interesting part is I remember studying. We took a bus there. It's about a seven-hour ride. I read a book for my history class about Russian history. And I think it was about the Soviet Union from 1917-1969. I just read it both ways all by myself. I was a dedicated student and I had to read this book. Talk about work.

Then we went to the Drake Relays. I had decided to run the mile that year to see what I could do because I had run an easy 2:56 ¾ mile in practice. With race adrenalin energy that might have translated into a four-minute mile. But something happened there. Not good. I went out in about 3:04. I finished up running 4:11. I just died in the last lap. One of those races where you just tie up and you can't do anything about it. You're just frozen with limbs burning from lack of enough oxygen flow. I think running that 2:56 four days before the race may have rung it out of me, although I felt really good on race day. I had hoped to run 4:04 and move up to the mile. I strongly believe I could have run a sub 4 minute mile. The season went on and a week or two later at home I ran the 880, and I broke the Northwestern record. I ran 1:49 (1:48.3 800 meters), way ahead with no competition all by myself in this meet against Loyola, DePaul, and a few local schools. I was feeling a little melancholy or sad that it was my last home race at the Northwestern track inside Dyche Stadium. But melancholy would hit me hard again that summer when my college track career at Northwestern ended after I graduated. Track had given me a place in life, somewhere I belonged and was successful, secure.

In May I went to the Big Ten Meet at Purdue, and I ran a disappointing fifth, about a 1:50.-something. Just didn't have it. But I did come back with my all-time best 400 meters equivalent, 46.7, in the relay. Bill Wehrwien, the champion MSU 440 runner, said I looked like I ran it like an all-out sprint. He was right. Years of strength work had paid off. But I was tired just like the year before, stale. You see, I peaked in that mid-February to mid-March time frame my junior and senior years. And by May, I was kind of strung out. I'd run a few good races in the spring, but I started to tire out, and I did less endurance training, more spot-on speed work here and there, quasi speed work, and being outside on the outdoor tracks all afternoon in the sun during large open track meets drained me. It just felt kind of hot and dry and dusty out there. When I went to the Central Collegiates at Notre Dame, I believe it was the next weekend, I ran another mediocre 1:50.5. But I had qualified for the NCAA by running the 1:49 in early May. So that was my best race, only really super good race of the outdoor season, besides the 2:56 ¾ mile in practice. Ron Kuchinski, my Michigan rival, said I should be running faster. He was right. And I did.

My sophomore year, I had peaked in mid-May and ran 1:49 at the Big Ten meet, first place. I had run 1:48 in April at the Drake Relays so I had a kind of second peak, we'll call it, for three weeks, late April to Mid-May. Then I got injured and I never came back in June. What usually happened is I'd come back in mid to late June for the NCAA and AAU meets and peak again, and sometimes with my best times. Usually for that three-week period at the end of May to early June there were no meets to speak of. So I went back to some lighter training, kind of a partial endurance period of running, some fartlek in flats and shorter quick distance runs, a few sandy beach runs, and a couple of moderate track workouts, like 8 x 220 or 3 x 440 at 27-29 220 pace, or 3 x 330 in 39-42 seconds, jog 330. Nothing fancy. My Junior year around this time I studied for finals at the one-mile long Lake Michigan beach (Wilmette Beach) with my girlfriend Robin. For study breaks I ran hard 2 mile runs in shallow one-foot water raising my legs and knees up and pushing hard. I did 2 sets of this for 3 days, just like my Rocky Balboa high school workouts. I strongly believe this really helped me 2 weeks later at the NCAA in Berkeley California. I usually came back in good form feeling recharged and ready to go. In those days there was a month between the Big Ten Meet and the NCAA-you could really lose your edge and feel lost from the world of competitive running. So in June 1968 at Berkeley I rebounded to finish 3rd in the 880 and make All American ranking. I loved CAL (Univerity of California) and Berkeley and San Francisco. Their energy and interesting open minded progressive people, inspiring land and ocean. I wish I had started my career there as a banker or bond trader. Cal Law School turned me down. Stanford business school said reapply when I get a little business experience, although I was admitted as an undergraduate.

WILMETTE BEACH RUN 1 mile each way

University of California Berkeley

Roosevelt Park Albuquerque built 1935 by USA work program, a good place to run in Albuquerque

So in my senior year I came back strong at the NCAA at the University of Tennessee. The temperature was close to 100 degrees and 90 percent humidity for three days in a row. I made the finals. I ran two races in the 1:48s. In the final I ran a 1:47.3, my best time by about a second, which is a 1:46.6 for 800 meters. But I only finished sixth because the winning time was 1:45.9, a new NCAA record. (Byron Dyce from Jamaica). 1:47 would have won in some other years. But that was the fastest 880-yard overall race in NCAA history. In other words, the gap between first and sixth place was the tightest and the fastest ever. If you added up all the first six times for places 1-6, it was the fastest NCAA 880 ever run. It was probably the fastest sixth place at 1:46.6 meters ever run. Only 1.4 seconds. Oh well, that's life.

Then we went down to the AAU meet in Miami, Florida. Some of us took a tour in the spectacular Everglades National Park. They have some real dangerous wildlife there so be careful. Big snakes, spiders, alligators, black panthers. I am so glad it is there, because it is losing its water and character due to commercial and agricultural expansion. It is always such a struggle to save nature when money talks. I didn't run well there. It was on national TV. I made the finals, but I think I didn't do a good job of warming down the prior day, and I just goofed it up again. That's my flaw in my psychology, my weakness. I lost a little focus socializing. Of course, I've learned now 45, 50 years later. That was the summer of '69. The end of my school boy competition. Very sad.

Everglades

Alligator in Everglades near Miami

Creature from The Black Lagoon 1956 movie. Scared? I was.

LAW SCHOOL STUDENT and UCTC NATIONAL 2-MILE RELAY CHAMPIONS-Summer 1969 to Spring 1970

RUNNING PATH PALOS FOREST PRESERVES

I would run fast 4-6 mile runs through these woods often accelerating the last mile all out. Very wonderful feeling and confidence and strength builder. Running should not always be tedious and organized. Let your body tell you how to run on any given day. How I wish I could just glide in there now, breaking a good sweat in the hot and humid weather. But I also ran here in the milder Autumn air. Very joyous and heading back home with a runner's high buzz.

Always try and run in places you love and that inspire you. Can you think of any? List them here.

University of Illinois 42,000 students ranked #14 in state universities. Where I went to Law school from_August 1969-February 1970

At the end of the June, the season ended, and I flew back to Chicago. Then I ran some of those University of Chicago Track Club meets at The University of Chicago in Hyde Park, an intellectual bastion of the world. I still like to walk around Hyde Park, looking at the buildings, shops, people, wondering what it would be like to live there. I always stop at Morry's Deli and the Valois Restaurant. They have been around for years and favorites of locals.

But I had the distinction of then working an awful part-time job at my friend's uncle's Italian grocery store on the South Side of Chicago. It was a little grocery story full of Italian people. A lot of little, old Italian ladies coming in there to buy all their green peppers. I stocked the vegetables and worked the cash register and the deli with all its pastrami cold cuts and cutting up various meats. Lucky I didn't cut off my fingers. I hated the job and driving down there at 9:00-ish in the morning, home by 5:00, 6:00 PM, exhausted, dispirited, hum drum life of a worker. I have respect, and I almost feel sorry for people who work labor. Most summers, I had to grind it out and make some money and got pushed into these awful boring tiring jobs. For workouts I started going over to nearby Brother Rice High School, a great Catholic high school. And of course, my favorite green forest paths. But what a come down for a super star working labor in an ethnic grocery store. A real bummer.

I was very melancholy after I left Northwestern that summer. I had a sense of loss and depression. I would go up to Evanston. A lot of times, I'd take the train, an hour and a half ride on the Chicago L (the elevated electric public train) and spend a night or two at my old apartment, which my roommate still had rented, and hang out with some of my old friends and fraternity brothers, and it was just like being in sort of a daze, I didn't know what to do with myself. I had been accepted to Georgetown Law School, one of the greatest law schools in the country, in Washington, DC, where I wanted to go because I also wanted to specialize in international relations and government work. And Georgetown was connected to all that. I went there with a friend of mine for a week before school started. I didn't know how I was going to pay for it. It was too expensive, and you had to live in an apartment. So about a week before school began, I applied to the University of Illinois Law School in Champaign-Urbana, got in and went down there at a much, much more reasonable price. I lived in Bromley Hall on the second floor with a bunch of other first-year law students. It was kind of fun. And practically the whole dorm was dedicated to undergrad Jewish kids from the Northern suburbs of Chicago and Rogers Park, which is nice. I got to know some of them. Sharp students. And I had no ambition for career or school whatsoever. Burned out. Just interested in running. *I would have been a good candidate for those track training camps I mentioned. But there were none.*

Bromley Hall, my residence in law school

So I arrived in the Fall at Champaign, Illinois about 150 miles south of Chicago in the middle of the Illinois farm belt. The area has some of the richest soil on earth for growing crops. And it is a rich dark black. It was a little warmer down there. I liked that and the big sprawling mega-campus with so much going on. I recollect -- I didn't like law school at all, and I was kind of lost academically. But running track kept me focused and somewhat stable. I remember running a Fall conditioning season on my own. And occasionally I'd run with some of the University of Illinois runners, not with the team, kind of solo here and there. It was about a mile or less to the track in Memorial Stadium from Bromley Hall. So I would walk and jog up there and then go over another half mile away to the University of Illinois farms and this gigantic field. It was about a half mile each way it seemed to me around the perimeter fence. I would run around the edge, kind of either a cross-country run or run like a half mile hard and a half mile easy, a half mile hard and a half mile easy. So I'd run that twice, which was four miles. And there was a golf course there too, on which I'd run fartlek, jogging and sprinting. One day after a golf course workout I stepped on the Memorial Stadium track and ran a 440 in 52 wearing flats (running shoes without spikes) by myself in this massive empty place where I had run 4 years before at the bustling Illinois State High School Meet. It was quite a contrast. Not a bad time, I still had good fitness and speed. Then on some days I would run west from Bromley Hall through the residential neighborhood, kind of in the central west side of Champaign and back again. It was just on the side streets. I remember I'd go out running kind of a medium pace and turn around and run all out all the way back down the sidewalk and street, altogether that was about a three mile run. Those were my key Fall workouts. I never ran all those 20 x 440 and 4 x 1 mile repetitive intervals. I hung out with my law student friends and talked about what we were going to do with our lives in the evening. I would study for a while and some evenings then go have a beer and a hot dog around the corner at this pinball place by the fraternity houses, and just generally kind of took it easy in that regard. I also went to a few crazy parties with some attractive dates, oh for the good old days! I developed a cozy temporary landing place, living and running there with my new friends from Chicago. I was still in the academic comfort zone, reflective, a haven from the cold cruel world lurking in the future. I was able to put that out of my mind. At times the melancholy would appear, I kind of savored it, and my friends and I shared our hopes, future plans, the world and the USA issues. I also went up to Northwestern a couple of time with my friends and hung out, dated a few of those nice senior co-eds. I had a nice smart attractive gal come down to visit me at Illinois. Her name was Nancy, an Alpha Phi. (sorority). She slept on an air mattress next to my bed. Her father was a high-ranking Admiral in the US Navy. Maybe I should have married her.

The Fall went by. I remember smoking cigars, these little Swisher Sweets, and trying to study. And, boy, was law school hard for me. I just didn't have it. Later on I found out the students called me The Phantom because I never went to many of the classes, but I still managed to get passing grades, mostly by cramming Gilbert's Notes over Christmas vacation. That bothered a friend of mine, because he went to class and studied hard each week, but all in good humor! But I did read the cases in the law textbooks and did a legal review research paper. My instructor said I was a good writer. Mentally I was in no man's land.

I think I may have run two cross-country races down there on roads by corn and soybean fields. I'm recollecting one was probably a six-miler, maybe both at so-so decent times, you know, not quite as fast as the year before at Northwestern. I wasn't training as hard. So my training was kind of ad hoc, edging off a little, but staying in shape. And I was a member of The University of Chicago Track Club, known as UCTC, and I was going to run in the 2-mile relay come winter. That was my new focus.

January came and I began to run track workouts after the Illinois track team finished about 5 PM in the Memorial Armory, which is where I set the world record the year before. I remember I got interviewed by the newspaper, and they did a nice write up about me, and the fact that I was going to law school there and what I had done the year before. And I ran again what I would call abbreviated workouts. It's hard to remember now, but I think they were shorter, speedier. Perhaps 8 to 10 x 220 in the 27 to 29 range, or some fast 330s around 39 to 43, maybe 5-6 of them.

But I know I did not run 10 x 440s or 20 x 220s or 4 x 880. More of the 220, 330, 440-yard moderate intense interval workouts with a little more emphasis on speed. I ran workouts that weren't the best for me to maximize my performance. So at least this got me in pretty good shape but not superb shape. I remember I ran in the three big time national indoor meets on the UCTC two-mile relay. We won all three, three weekends in a row in February. I flew on a non-stop flight, a small jet, a DC 9 out of Champaign-Urbana non-stop to La Guardia Airport on Ozark Airlines. And that was really fun. We'd all arrive the day before and stay across Madison Square Garden in an old-line kind of rustic old hotel (The New Yorker), but clean and respectable, and meet all the athletes, have a nice dinner. The meets were at night, and we won the two mile relay each weekend, three in a row. How great to still be nationally at the top. The meets were the Olympic Invitational, then the following week was the famous Millrose Games, and that was on television. And then the National AAU, which is now named the USA Track and Field Federation national meet. We won that as well. So we were famous. A warm fulfilling sense of accomplishment and pride. I was on top again. Looking back I was very fortunate. Over six seasons since I turned 18, I was in first place 14 times in major meets by myself or on a relay team. Three American records. After 9 years of success, FAME had become my addiction and emotional support. I forget how outstanding that was. Today, things are tough, modest, and humble. So respect the unfortunate, the low income folks. Think of helping someone as an honor, maybe even a duty. When I had money and lived on the Pine Ridge Indian Reservation I sprinkled it around. It is a great feeling to give money away to help people and for good causes. That's a great thing about money, the satisfaction of giving it away.

But I wasn't a saint either. I am not broke nor in poverty but financially precarious due to enrollment declines and course cutbacks.

Anyway, back to indoor track. My teammates were Lowell Paul, who was our number one runner, who went to the University of Kansas, became a lawyer and went to University of Chicago Law School, a brilliant intellectual liberal guy. Ken Sparks and I were vying for second and third. Ken went to Ball State, got a PhD and worked at Cleveland Clinic as a researcher in physiology. Bob O'Connor was our lead-off man and a tad slower than the rest of us, but slim and agile. He gave us a lead more often than not. He was a graduate of Loyola University and went on to get a PhD there and has become a private practice psychologist.

In February 1970 I dropped out of law school at the University of Illinois. It just was not for me. Besides I had no ambition after a 4 year grind as a college student athlete-just totally burned out and feeling lost. All I wanted to do was run in meets. The corporate working world seemed threatening to me, an alien place full of hard nosed business people without the sensitivities and ideals I had developed from a very eye opening intense liberal arts education. I had no, zero, interest in working for the sole purpose of making money. Besides in my heart I was a rebellious student. In November 1969 I was in the new draft lottery and my number came up #20. For certain I would be drafted into the army and possibly sent to Vietnam. I was very upset and concerned. I wasn't about to be killed in a foolish war one-half of the US people didn't believe in. The Army had a track team, but I was concerned I might lose my ability or slip through the cracks and be bypassed and sent to 'Nam. See the movies Platoon and Full Metal Jacket for a real good look at that war. It would take a year to get drafted. A law school friend, Jack, a regular guy from Cicero, a moderate income old eastern European ethnic Chicago suburb and mafia controlled in the past, became a criminal public defender lawyer. We took an inspired trip (more like a quest) to New York City-Manhattan and Boston to visit his sisters and see the cities. We listened to songs by Janis Joplin, Canned Heat, Jefferson Airplane, Led Zeppelin, Simon and Garfunkel, and the inspiring and sentimental song Massachusetts by the Bee Gees (over and over) all the way there. And hey, don't forget Bob Dylan (Lay Lady Lay). Of course we also went to Harvard to see and feel the intellectual rebellious buzz. One sister in Manhattan was a young advertising executive, so we slept on her apartment floor. We spent all day walking around Manhattan, past the United Nations, fascinated by the enormous bustling city, the center of the USA. Another sister taught at an elite upper-class girls boarding school in Greenwich, Connecticut. There we saw a glimpse into the world of the wealthy, the future women leaders of our country and maybe the world. Or married into it. All the way we pondered our fate, discussing how we would ever fit into American mainstream society. Being in school seemed to be the haven where we fit and were comfortable, our safe place. Oh, and that Fall we took part in an anti-Vietnam peaceful march carrying candles, singing Judy Collins songs. And splash! A garbage can full of water cane pouring down on me from the student second floor dorm. Not everyone at the University of Illinois shared our sensitivities. After I left Illinois I was accepted at The University of Chicago Graduate Business School in finance. I had to do something, but what and for why I did not know. Just keep competing now for the University of Chicago Track Club and stay a student, something I liked and was good at. Full of hope. All of us liberal students in the entire country shared a common bond, it was comforting and inspiring too. We were out to remake the world better, as we saw it, and reshape the cultural values of the USA. Little did we know that the world and the USA would reshape us instead.

Then we ran some individual meets as well here and there and at The University of Chicago. That season would end in mid-March at the Central AAU meet. I remember that year running a 600-yard run, which was an indoor race which is basically a 440-yard sprint and you hang on. I ran about two steps behind Lowell Paul all the way, and I think he ran about a 1:09.7, and I ran a 1:10.4. Pretty good times. But to me, it was just an all out guts run that really kind of tore me up. I wouldn't want to run that type of race on a regular basis. UCTC won the NAAU 2 Mile Relay 8 out of 9 years from 1969-1977. The 1971 team I was on ran 7:28.6, a record that lasted until 1992. Quite a feat. Go look it up. I usually ran about 1:52-1:53 on the slower 11 lane board track with very sharply banked turns. Boards aren't run anymore. But they were more exciting than today's rubber surface 200 and 300 meter boring ovals. Track is not what it once was, despite outstanding performances.

In the winter, I dropped out of law school, and I became a high school substitute teacher in the spring in the City of Chicago at Altgeld Gardens. I didn't last long. Today that section of the city has a very high gang murder rate. And then I became a substitute teacher at Oaklawn High School and at Evergreen Park High School most of the time, my alma mater. I trained again, and I ran outdoor track for UCTC. I remember flying out to the Quantico Relays at the Marine base in Virginia and running all sorts of relays there. We went to the Ohio State Relays and I finished second to Andy O'Reilly in the 880, the former Villanova star, and ran some relay races as well. We ran a dual meet outdoors at the University of Michigan. We ran at the Eastern Michigan Relays, the Western Michigan Relays. We ran a dual meet at the University of Wisconsin at Madison. I remember these well. It's a little bit hazy in my mind, the different meets we went to during the spring of 1970 through 1971. I was starting to slow down a little bit too. In 1971 we won the three major 2- mile relay races in NYC again, beating the New York Athletic Club by one-tenth of a second in the NAUU Championship. We won the at the Penn Relays, and were second at The Martin Luther King Games won by the Kenyan National Team--a distinction to run against such great athletes.

BRIAN OLDFIELD-the GREAT SHOT PUTTER

Sadly, Brian passed away last year at the age of 72. He competed for UCTC in the shot put and I got to know him well. He made the Olympic team in 1972 and set a world record. He was both fun to be with and a fiercely competitive athlete. He had thrown the shot some of the longest distances in the world and created new throwing techniques. He appeared on the cover of Sports Illustrated magazine in a skimpy Speedo swimming suit in USA red white and blue stripes. At the national meet he smoked a cigarette in between throws. They say that psyched out Randy Mattson, the world's best then, who clutched and lost to Brian! We traveled as roommates on a trip to the University of Michigan. In July of 1969 we went to the Central AAU meet in Sterling Illinois, an all-day relays event with athletes of all abilities. We met two TWA flight attendants who were meet helpers and had a wonderful evening, all four of us together.

UCTC 2 Mile Relay Summer 1970

My training regime was mostly to run in Oak Lawn because I worked and came home (I lived with my parents when in Graduate School) and then I would run in this nearby athletic field park, which was about 600 yards around, a really kind of intense fartlek for about three miles of jogging, striding hard, short distances, 200 meters, 400 meter bursts. Other days I would drive back out to the Palos Forest Preserves and cruise a fast 4-5 mile run, smooth and with good flow. It's a surprise to most people that the Chicago area has these extensive dense woods, small lakes, and trails near the city. And once or twice a week, I'd go to the track down at The University of Chicago. I'd drive down there after school, get there about 4:30 in the afternoon, and run again these modified interval workouts. Once I ran an all-out 440 in 49, and that was my workout. You see, Zeus Preckwinkle was running interval 440s in about 60 and he didn't realize how fast I was running, and he tried to run with me, and I left him in the dust. He still talks about it to this day jokingly. His wife, Toni Preckwinkle, has been President of the Cook County Board for the past 6 years, a tremendous elected job in Chicago, the third most powerful position in the State of Illinois behind the Governor and the Mayor. Or perhaps equal to the Mayor of the City of Chicago.

1970--Ready to pass Zeus Preckwinkle running 2-mile relay leg at University of Chicago Track Club Meet 1.49.6. Picture is old and blurry.

Zeus has moved to the Philippines and still runs long distances. By the way the country is the 7th fastest growing economy of the world developing nations.

So my workouts then were runs of three to four 400s in the mid to upper 50s (55-59) or sometimes six to eight 200s, 25 to 28 (mostly 26-27). So again I started doing, what I call, lazy man's workouts, kind of the more speedy stuff, abbreviated, and I was kind of short on training time. And it showed in my times, which were good but I wasn't quite in as good as shape as I was the prior two years. I was running around 1:50 for 800 meters, give or take. And I did qualify by running a 1:49 880 in May at the University of Chicago Track Club Stagg Field open meet they had every May. I qualified for the National AAU (USATF today) in Bakersfield, California, near the end of June.

It was a lot of fun there. I met again Keith Colburn, who I had gotten to know. He was my age, a graduate from Harvard. I'd run against him on and off over a few years. We had a lot in common. His family lived in Hollywood in a residential area just off Sunset Strip up in a very nice residential area. I stayed there with him a few days. We both ran at Bakersfield, California in the National AAU Meet, and I qualified for the final, ran about a 1:48.2 800-meter equivalent (1.48.9 880) and felt good in the final. I finished sixth, but my race time was very good. I was only about a second and a half behind first place (actually 1.7 seconds). We were all bunched up together. Sixth place counted and I won a medal and got some official points for UCTC. So I ran well, but I was just not quite on to my 1:47 times. I was pretty close considering I didn't run as much, and I'd put on about five pounds. So I was happy with that.

Keith and I drove back to LA over the dry desolate Santa Monica mountains. Surprising that just on the other side was the sprawling metropolis of LA. There I explored UCLA in Westwood and also visited with my college friend Sue Palmer at her parents' home in Belair overlooking the city. Nice people. Interestingly, a movie agent took me on a tour through a movie studio.

Outdoors 1969 Northwestern, receiving baton mile relay 48.2

There I met three movie stars filming on their sets. Peter Graves, the star of Mission Impossible, the spectacular television series, Florence Henderson, and Milton Berle, an icon of TV comedy He was a gruff and impressive person, larger than life. Sometimes today I wish I had stayed out there and become a movie star, lived the good life, been famous and in the hubbub of the entertainment business. Here we go again, attention and applause.

That summer of '70 was a big highlight of my track career, although I did compete another year. But I was starting to peak out. But it was great after running that beautiful sixth place finish in Bakersfield, California, and then spending a few days in LA afterwards. Then I went back to Chicago. I didn't have a miserable summer job thank goodness.

The angst started again which has bothered me on and off my entire life. I have to say that today I still feel a sense of angst, that despite making huge efforts to be successful and fit into American life, I have a regret that my life has been unfulfilled. But most people don't have the intense experience of living with American Indians or teaching economics to moderate income students full of hope to succeed and break into mainstream middle-class society. I inspire them. Maybe that is why I am becoming a writer.

Oh, but I want to add that as I have mentioned when I was 18 years I worked on an experimental color picture tube assembly line as a data collector for Motorola during July. In 1965 color televisions were just getting developed. Boring, but for 6 weeks I was part of the great American labor force and the expansion of the American economy. I also read several Ian Fleming James Bond 007 novels during breaks. Remember those great movies starring Sean Connery and a cast of villains and beautiful women?

I continued my moderate interval workouts, and I ran in the weekly summer meets at The University of Chicago. They were weekly from the end of June till the end of July. And then to my great surprise and delight, in mid-July, several of us got called to a national training camp at the University of Oregon in Eugene, Oregon. For most of us, we weren't the superstar athletes. I would call us the second tier. Those who had finished fourth, fifth, sixth nationally, or really good regionally, were invited out there. Why? I don't know. The top athletes were in Europe running the big meets. I guess this was an experiment to build depth, and it was a good idea. We need more of these training camps. This is the type of group I want to train and coach, and for which this book is directed, taking these athletes to a higher level of performance.

So somewhere towards the end of July I was flown out to Eugene, Oregon. Lowell Paul was there, my friend from the University of Chicago Track Club, and other people I'd kind of gotten to know over a couple of years in my event. Marcel Philippe in the 880, Larry LeMaster, from the University of South Dakota team, and many others, especially Oregon distance runners. I was sort of in awe of them. I think Bob Seagram the Olympic pole vaulter was there. And so what we did is we stayed in the dorms. You can still see them by the current track. It looks the same. And I don't remember the workouts exactly. But I do remember the morning runs, which I wasn't crazy about. But we would run about three miles at a pretty good clip about 8:00 in the morning. I had a hard time keeping up. And then we ran some, it seemed to me, moderate interval workouts in the late afternoon. And I just can't quite remember what they all are. But again, they weren't the heavy speed and endurance ones I had run at Northwestern. I'm trying to remember. We probably ran five or six 400s in the upper 50s, or eight 200s in 26-29. Or a few 300's in 39-42. Or perhaps a 660 in 1:21-1:22. Those type of workouts. Of course, we only had three weeks. The middle weekend, we were there about a week, we went to Honeyman State Park on the Oregon Coast. There are gigantic sand hills right along the ocean. We ran up and down them. It was beautiful and challenging. And then I remember walking along the long beach and seeing seals jumping in and out of the water, swimming about 100 feet out from the shore. It was a gray day. And it was kind of slightly rough surf. It was awe-inspiring. The ocean and beach looked like they were to be taken seriously, not playful at all.

Then we ran for another week. During the week some of the routine was that after a day of running we walked into town, around campus, talked. A little boring, but also interesting. I did some reading. We did take a trip on a Sunday up in the mountains for some activities. And then in the evenings, after we ate dinner, sometimes I'd go downtown with some of the guys. We had a bar/restaurant we liked to have some beers in, spend a few hours shooting the bull. I met a gal there, who I kind of liked and spent some time with her in town. And at the culmination at the end of two weeks, we ran an exhibition track meet, but it was unofficial. But believe it or not, four of us put together a two-mile relay team that set an American record of about 7:16, which is about a 7:14 at 4 x 800 meters, not a shabby time. Marcel Philippe was on that team, and Dean Bierke of the US Army. I ran the third leg in 1:49. Our anchor Lowell Paul, ran about 1:48. We were applauded and complimented for that. We had no competition. Since it was unofficial it never was really put in the record books. But I have some articles from the newspapers

about it in Track and Field News. I think about it to this day. It was totally unexpected. Great to be a winner. Are you a winner?

Lowell Paul 2008 Topeka Kansas Public Defender Attorney

READERS NOTES: What does it take to be a winner, your ideas only.

American two-mile relay mark falls in twilight meet

EUGENE, OREGON JULY 1970

By BUD WITHERS
Of the Register-Guard

Lowell Paul's unofficial 1:48.2 anchor leg carried four Olympic preparation camp half-milers to a new American record of 7:16.2 in the two-mile relay Saturday night in a twilight track meet at Hayward Field.

The bearded Paul, who did his undergraduate running for the University of Kansas and since has graduated from Chicago Law School, and Marcel Philippe of Fordham, Dean Bjerke of Army and Ralph Schultz of the Chicago Track Club combined to better the listed American mark of 7:17.4 set by a University of Southern California quartet in 1966.

The twilight meet climaxed the three-week Olympic preparation camp for middle distance runners, steeplechasers and intermediate hurdlers held at the University of Oregon under U.S. Olympic Committee auspices.

Paul, who now runs for the Chicago Track Club and is scheduled to leave soon for Germany to begin a study of German law on a fellowship, had a five-yard lead on Denis Flood of Tennessee at the outset of the anchor leg and poured it on for the final two laps. The runner-up team of half-milers from the Olympic camp finished in 7:22.5.

"I was getting tired, but I'm in as good shape as I ever was," Paul said afterwards.

Paul said he thought the world record of 7:14.6 (held by West Germany) was out of reach, but knew well he had a chance at the U.S. mark.

Among other things, the meet featured a swift steeplechase event and program-ending mile run that ended in a tie.

Mike McClendon, a sophomore-to-be (athletically) at Oregon, ended the hectic mile in a 4:00.7 dead heat with Dennis Savage of Westmont (Calif.) College.

McClendon, only 18, was a Duck sophomore last spring, but was redshirted because of a knee injury.

Steve Savage, UO steeplechase star and no relation to the runnerup, led after 2½ laps and was still in front as they passed the three-quarter mark in 3:03.

At this point, Dennis Savage burst into the lead, but McClendon, moving fast from third place on the backstretch, caught first Steve and then Dennis. As they came off the final turn, McClendon moved a few inches in front, but Dennis Savage pulled even in the last few yards to the tape.

McClendon had figured earlier the two- or three-mile was his best race. "That's what I thought before tonight," he grinned. "But with Prefontaine there, I might be a miler." His previous personal best for the mile was 4:11.2.

Dennis Savage praised McClendon's performance afterwards.

"Everybody was scared of him (McClendon) all week," the Californian said. "He was running us into the ground. He's really doing well."

Bill Norris of the U. S. Army and 1969 AAU champion Mike Manley gave the estimated crowd of 2,000 its first batch of excitement with a rousing battle in the steeplechase.

Manley spurted to an early 25-30 yard lead, but Norris cut the deficit in half with about two laps to go.

At the gun lap, the two were neck-and-neck, but Norris caught Manley with about 220 yards to go and won by 10 yards.

"Warming up I had a bad cramp in my side," Norris noted later, "but I felt all right during the race."

Norris said he almost gave up track after a disappointing sickness at the AAU championships in Bakersfield, Calif., earlier this summer.

"I was fed up with track," he recounted, "but you just have to bounce back."

He cited the Olympic camp as the force that kept him around. "There was no real pressure here and the video tape machine really helped me."

Norris will complete his tour of Army duty in December and hopes to return to finish graduate work on a business degree at the UO, as well as continue running.

In the high jump, Marty Hill of the UO topped 6-10 and beat a field of high school jumpers, led by Salem's Mike Fleer at 6-8.

Other highlights:

Larry Kreider of the Navy breezed to a win in the 440 intermediate hurdles in 52.2, while Tim Bishop of Churchill claimed the 330 intermediates with a 42.3 clocking.

TRACK

Twilight Meet At Hayward Field

70-YARD DASH (Girls 6 and under)—1, Karen Kryzanowski, 12.1. 2, Robyn Yarham, 12.6. 3, Cindy Barker, 12.7.

70-YARD DASH (Boys 6 and under)—1, Glenn Smith, 11.1. 2, Craig Dickerson, 11.3. 3, Peter Stevens, 11.6.

70-YARD DASH (Girls 7 and 8)—1, Denise Zeibert, 10.6. 2, Laura Merrill, 10.8. 3, Jackie Aiken, 11.2.

70-YARD DASH (Boys 7 and 8)—1, Roger Daniels, 10.7. 2, Lynn Couch, 10.9. 3, Chris Holden, 11.0.

HIGH SCHOOL JAVELIN—1, Dennis Durham, Marshall, 221-9. 2, Steve Hopkins, Grant, 210-1½. 3, Dave Melville, Enterprise, 205-7. 4, Rick Davis, Central Linn, 203-5½.

3,000 METER STEEPLECHASE—1, Bill Norris, Army, 8:47.6. 2, Mike Manley, Oregon Track Club, 8:49.1. 3, Jon Anderson, 9:03.1.

100-YARD DAHS (Girls)—1, Wanda Taylor, Springfield, 11.1. 2, Susan George, Brownsville, 11.3. 3, Julie Ward, Gresham, 11.6.

220-YARD DASH (Girls 9 and 10)—1, Carol Huey, 30.3. 2, Sian Leyshon, 32.2. 3, Anne Moore, 32.3.

220-YARD DASH (Boys 9 and 10)—1, Greg Hanson, 30.7. 2, Paul Geary, 30.8. 3, Erik Guldager, 31.2.

330-INTERMEDIATE HURDLES—1, Tim Bishop, Churchill, 42.3. 2, Roger Hall, Ashland, 42.4. 3, Skip Bunson, Corvallis, 43.1.

440-INTERMEDIATE HURDLES—1, Larry Kreider, Navy, 52.2. 2, Jim Herndon, East Oklahoma State, 55.5. 3, Dan Caram, Midwest City HS, Okla., 56.0.

HIGH JUMP—1, Marty Hill, Oregon, 6-10. 2, Mike Fleer, McNary, 6-8. 3, (tie) Dennis Durham, Marshall, and Mike Buss, Central, 6-2. POLE VAULT—1, Dan Hedges, Oregon, 15-0. 2, Jim Dowhower, South Eugene HS, 14-6. 3, Terry Shortesign, Reedsport, 14-0.

880 (Girls)—1, Sherry Wells, Springfield, 2:22.2. 2, Cheryl Bates, 2:24.7. 3, Tary Mitchell, 2:27.1.

TWO-MILE RELAY—1, Olympic Training Team No. 1 (Marcel Philippe, Fordham; Dean Bjerke, Army; Ralph Schultz, Chicago Track Club; Lowell Paul, Chicago Track Club), 7:16.2. 2, Olympic Training Team No. 2 (Roger Colglazier, Abilene Christian; Rick Brown, Los Altos, Calif.; Larry Lemaster, Army; Denis Flood, Tennessee), 7:22.5. (Betters American record of 7:17.4 set by USC, 1966).

MILE—1, (tie) Mike McClendon, Oregon and Dennis Savage, Westmont College, 4:00.7; 3, Steve Savage, Oregon, 4:05.3.

ATTENDANCE—2,000 (est.)

Then I stuck around for another day or two and went home back to reality in Chicago. Summer was going by and to my incredible surprise, within a week or less, Ted Haydon called me and said, "You've been selected to run on an American team in Europe." Brooks Johnson was the coach. It must have been about 15 athletes. And again, we weren't the top tier athletes. We were, what I'd call, the second tier, except for Willie White, who went on the trip, and was on 5 Olympic teams, and from Chicago and

competed for the Mayor Daley Youth Foundation. Her event was the long jump. But most of all, we were very good but not the superb super elite US athletes. So they flew us out for a week. We went to Wuppertal, West Germany, which is not far from Düsseldorf, for a meet. And the funny part is being German, I was given a special welcome by the mayor and his daughter and driven all over town sightseeing. I was considered the German American. So with the name of Ralph Schultz, I got a newspaper headline with a picture of me, the mayor, and his daughter. I thought that was rather amusing. I was also proud of my heritage and felt honored. And I also had a special ride to and from the meet in a Mercedes sedan. And again, I ran a mediocre 1:50, you know, about fifth out of eight or nine runners. And for some reason I just didn't have it. I was wearing out. I was ending the long summer tired over my peak whereas the Europeans were in the middle of their racing season in top form. I wish I could have run faster for the Germans. We had a banquet after the Meet, and I always remembered what the Englishman at my table said about the Germans, that as soon as they hear a marching band they all line up in formation. WWII had ended only 25 years prior. England and Germany had been major enemies.

Then we flew to Barcelona and spent a few days there and ran the 800m again. I ran about the same type of lackluster race and time. I remember walking up and down their plaza and the street with all its small, beautiful shops. We all had a nice time there. We saw a bullfight. They butcher the bull right there after it is killed by the matador. It is brutal. Then we flew back on Pan Am to New York and to Chicago. And by that time, it was the fall. It was early September.

Wuppertal Newspaper. Me, John Craft, and Mayor's Daughter. The Germans were very proud.

onnerstag, 24. September 1970

Abendsportfest: Die ersten Asse sind schon da

Die ersten prominenten Teilnehmer für das Internationale Abendsportfest im Stadion (ab 18.30 Uhr) trafen bereits gestern in Wuppertal ein. Schon hier sind die dänische 800-m-Spezialistin,

US-Mittelstreckler Rolf Schulz. 800-m-Bestzeit: 1:46,6 Min.

Anneliese Damm-Olesen, US-Sprinter Charlie Smith und sein Landsmann Rolf Schulz (800 m).

Alle anderen Teilnehmer kamen bereits in der vergangenen

Zweite bei den Europameisterschaften, Anneliese Damm-Olesen

Nacht nach Wuppertal, oder treffen im Laufe des Tages ein.

Bis zum gestrigen Nachmittag hatte Organisator Paul Schlurmann 100 Sportler-Zusagen.

US-Sprinter-Star Charlie Smith. Er lief die 200 m in 20,7 Sek.

Der 101. Teilnehmer rief am frühen Abend an: Volker Ohl, Deutscher Stabhochsprungmeister (5,20 m).

Zwei Amerikaner in Wuppertal

Erste Gäste des Abendsportfestes trafen ein

Der Hauch des „Sportlich-Internationalen" wehte bereits gestern durch Wuppertal. Das 14. Internationale Abendsportfest begrüßte seine ersten Gäste. Die Silbermedaillen-Gewinnerin bei den Europameisterschaften in Athen, die Dänin Anneliese Damm-Olesen, reiste aus Versehen einen Tag zu früh aus Kopenhagen an und nahm so den Begrüßungstrunk zusammen mit den beiden Amerikanern Chuck Smith und Rolf Schulz ein.

Über das bis zuletzt ungewisse Kommen der beiden amerikanischen Läufer freute sich Paul Schlurmann, Organisator des Leichtathletik-Abendsportfestes, natürlich besonders. Der farbige Chuck Smith wird über die 100 und 200 Meter starten und nach Schlurmanns Voraussage beide Rennen siegreich gestalten. Hervorragend ist die Zeit des Amerikaners mit dem deutschen Namen. Rolf Schulz läuft die 800 Meter in 1:46,6 Minuten und wird seinen Start in Wuppertal, trotz guter Konkurrenz, sicherlich ebenfalls siegreich beenden.

● Letzte Verpflichtung: Der Deutsche Stabhochsprungmeister Volker Ohl wird in Wuppertal ebenfalls dabei sein.

● Das Abendsportfest findet bei jeder Witterung statt.

Die Ersten, die in Wuppertal ankamen und die Favoriten ihrer Starts: Anneliese Damm-Olesen und die beiden Amerikaner Rolf Schulz und Chuck Smith.

Foto: Peter Reis

UCTC 2 MILE RELAY NATIONAL CHAMPIONS 1971-Graduate Business School Fall 1970--Summer 1971-Bob O'Connor (Loyola U.); Ken Sparks (Ball State); Me (Northwestern); Lowell Paul (Kansas U.)

CTC'S United States AAU two mile relay champions. l. to r. Bob C
en Sparks, Ralph Schultz, Lowell Paul.

jumped 16-6 to win the pole vault, John Craft
51-7 3/4 to win the triple jump, Bill Cuello was s

Well, by that time I had been admitted to The University of Chicago Graduate School of Business on the South Side [Fall `1970]. And I really was proud of myself and I still am that I graduated from there. They are called the Maroons, the nickname for the undergraduates and the school color. It's a fantastic school. And though I'm proud of Northwestern, something about The University of Chicago and its international excellence in all sorts of fields is just unparalleled. The Graduate Business School is one of the best in the country. Now it's been ranked one of the best in the world here in 2017 by The Economist a magazine respected worldwide. That was 1970. So I majored in finance, that was Chicago's big thing, not knowing what I really wanted to do, except I was always interested in economics. And I thought some job in the investment business or the Federal Government, would suit me just fine.

University of Chicago along the beautiful Midway Plaisance

Then it was Fall 1970. I didn't really run cross-country. I just ran medium effort workouts, not real hard nor long in distance. I would run three or four mile runs in the neighborhood fairly hard, sometimes solid straight through, sometimes breaking it up into speed play and fartlek, and sometimes I went out to the forest preserves in Palos Park again that I loved dearly and still do and ran 4-6 miles at 5-6 minutes a mile. That was about 20-25 miles a week. In fact, I ran in the Palos Woods this past summer of 2017 (at age 70), along Long John Slough a (marshy lake) and on the beautiful horse riding trails and wood chip paths that I had run 45 years before. It brought back memories and was delightful. I ran-walked about 2 miles at 13-15 minutes per mile, worked up a good sweat in the summer heat. Ahhhhhh, it felt good. It was a good time. I can only remember running one or two cross-country meets in November with The University of Chicago Track Club in Washington Park. It was mostly just a conditioning period. And I had to study hard you know. I commuted from my parent's home in Oak Lawn where I now lived. It was about a 30 minute drive to Hyde Park. I parked on the Midway Plaisance, a beautiful very wide boulevard built during the Columbian Exposition of 1893. At one mile long and 220 yards wide, it runs through The University of Chicago and connects two major parks, Washington and Jackson. I always considered it a special place since I was a little boy growing up 4 miles away. It was my mother's route that took us to the Jackson Park Beach in 1950-54. I was at the University all day, two or three days a week, taking classes and studying, then running a workout.

Just to let you know how disciplined I was and how hard it was, I actually had all my classes on two days a week, either Monday and Wednesday or Tuesday, Thursday. And the other three days I worked as a substitute teacher mostly at Evergreen Park High School, occasionally at Oak Lawn and Reavis. But I used that time to study because in those days students behaved and they were quiet. And while they did their assignment, I could do my schoolwork, so it worked out just fine. I didn't have many problems with the students. Strange, isn't it? Times change. I got an A in Linear Programming, a difficult math optimization course, and was about mid-point academically at school.

So anyway, track season came up in January. And again, I had that same tough schedule. So what I would do is, let's for instance say, on Monday and Wednesday I scheduled my classes. They were done by mid-afternoon. Then I would go over to the fieldhouse in the wintertime and run a track workout at 4:00 or 5:00 in the afternoon after I had studied all day, been there since 9:00 in the morning. And I was tired. And again, I think these were, what I would call, the more abbreviated workouts, 8-10 x 220 in 27-30 seconds, 440's in the mid 50's, a few of those.

Sometimes a 3/4 mile occasionally followed by 2 x 220 fairly fast, 25-26. I also ran an all-out 330 in 37. That's when a coach watching me said I should be a miler. I don't remember the workouts very well unfortunately. But, as I have said, they weren't so hard like two years before. They were more like tuning workouts. They really weren't to build the super strength endurance necessary to run championship times. But they did the job for our relay team and qualified me for the nationals later that year. I had put on another five pounds so I was up about eight or 10 from my prime running weight. I was slowing down. I could still slug out a good split on the two-mile relay. And I'd become a 1:50 to 1:51 half miler instead of a 1:48 half miler, which is not bad but not really fantastic.

So we again ran a similar indoor season. I think that we did run at the Western Michigan and Eastern Michigan Relays again. We did the February routine, this time flying from O'Hare or Midway to New

York City. We'd fly Friday and run on Saturday night. And as in the prior year, we won the Olympic Invitational, the Millrose Games and the National AAU Indoor Meet. So we had won six big races in a row over two years. Quite a feat. After I left the team that year, the University of Chicago Track Club went on to win four more years in a row with Rick Wohlhuter joining the team, the world record holder from St. Charles, Illinois, who ironically enough I'd beaten in high school by about a second two different times. So anyway, that was the indoor season, exciting and enjoyable, being with great athletes and friends, winning and being well known. We also competed against some Big Ten schools. I remember driving up to The University of Michigan with Brian Oldfield, the great Olympian shot putter, laughing and swapping stories. He recently passed away at age 72. He will be missed and was admired and loved by all. The past few years he wrote many messages on Facebook about his track and field experiences and advanced training methods. In his prime he was 6-6 and 270 pounds of muscle. He could outrun many sprinters and dunk a basketball from a standing position. We used to stop at a great well-known old-time Prime Rib restaurant, Win Schuler's, outside Kalamazoo, Michigan. Ted picked up the tab.

US ARMY LOGO

US War Room World Center

By this time, I had joined the US Army Reserves in the Fall of 1970. I went to meetings on Monday nights. And that took up some extra time and energy and planning.

I had a Top Secret Umbra security clearance and was a geo-political strategic analyst. My small unit wrote a major yearly report about some international issue. In August we went to the Pentagon to finish it with all the secret intelligence we were provided. The Cold War was on.

So in the spring of 1971 we again ran in some meets in the mid-west and out East. University of Wisconsin and Michigan, Penn Relays, and then an outdoor meet at The University of Chicago Open where again, as the year prior year, I ran the 1:49 qualifying time for the outdoor NAUU Meet at the University of Oregon, a good time that surprised me. Well, I just didn't have it by then. A month had transpired, and I just ran a lousy preliminary time of about 1:51 again and was eliminated. And just two weeks after that I went to basic training in the Army to learn to become a soldier. And believe it or not, I set the Fort Ord one-mile run basic raining record of 4:52, running in combat boots, a T-shirt, and Army khaki pants. The commanding officer, the Captain, gave our platoon a case of beer. He was so happy and proud that it was his Company. So in that summer I was in the Army at basic training at Fort Ord, California. And believe it or not, I would still sometimes run sprints in the open area next to the barracks after the good Army evening chow. Crazy yes, but fun. And still thinking about our relay team and the upcoming meets in the winter.

THE ENDING-Fall 1971-Arizona

Then we were flown to advanced individual training at Fort Huachuca, Arizona. That's where all the very top-secret army communications training occurs. That's no secret. They had a 440-yard outdoor track there. I was still trying to run some interval workouts and then do some light distance running near the mountains, down this lonely road. And that was the end for me. It was around early October on a beautiful 75-degree early evening, the sun was still out. I was running about a three-mile easy run, plodding along, and my legs didn't have any bounce. And I stopped, and I looked in this beautiful valley where the sun was setting, a V cut in the mountains. And those mountains went up to 10,000 feet, sometimes had snow on top in the Fall. I was in the flat area leaving the post, heading south. And I said, "That's it. I quit. I'm done." And it was over just like that. So ten years before, I started running. I remember when John Megson, my high school coach, pointed to me and said, "I want you out for track," that was the instantaneous beginning. And strangely enough, it was an instantaneous end. I find that quite interesting and also ironic. What do you guys and gals think?

Oh, I have to tell you about 2 adventures I did. One Sunday at Ft Huachuca 8 of us piled into two cars and drove 5 hours to the Grand Canyon. Got there about noon. It's a 5-mile switchback trail to the bottom by the wild fast-moving Colorado River. I ran most of it. At the bottom we rested and had some water at the closed Phantom Ranch. I was fascinated looking at this mighty ancient river. Then up we went with no water! Well, I'll you, we found out in a hurry that going up is a lot lot harder than going down. We walked up for 3 hours. Towards the top we were so exhausted we crawled on our hands and knees for 5 minutes and then rested for 5 minutes. And the sun was getting low. Well we made it and drove 6 hours back to the Fort getting there at 1 AM. Can you believe it, the exertion? An Amazing feat!! I also hiked way up the Huachuca mountains myself to the snow line, about 2 hours. And guess what? Bear tracks all over the place. Another one of my adventures, just like in my childhood with my friends.

So my track career ended. I went back to Chicago in November 1971. For years I still ran in some of the 5K and 10K weekend meets. And I was still trying to do my best and be competitive although at slower times for my age and less training. But I pushed it on and off since then to today. My 5K time went from 15 to 44 minutes over 45 years. I no longer compete in races. In 1992 at age 45 I ran some 5k's in 20-21 minutes, and many weekend 5 k's all over Chicagoland. And a few 10k's. Best time was 46:30. It was

fun running out there for so many minutes, being part of this runner's fraternity. It gave me something meaningful to do on Saturday and Sunday morning, an adventure into new places. I remember I ran a 4:52 mile around the Reservoir in Central Park in New York City in 1977.

So what happened is through my whole life, I've run on and off, and even now at my age of 70. I've run in 5Ks in my 60s, ran 36 minutes a few times at age 62. But the last couple years, I realized it's just not a good idea to run that hard. So I run--walk one and a half to three miles four days a week. The Fall of 2016 I worked out 49 days in a row. In 2017 I went 82 days. I set a record for myself, another adventure. My blood cholesterol reading dropped to 133! Occasionally, I do two to four miles at the golf course on a running trail. One-half is hilly. About 29-30 minutes for a 2-mile run at 5000-foot altitude. Push it up the hills. I might walk two and run one or two miles around 45-60 minutes. Yes, it's high here in New Mexico. I'm not terribly out of breath when I run. I just can't get those legs moving. I guess I need an inspiration, or new legs! This gives me great satisfaction and builds self-esteem, at a time when other aspects of my life are fading. I can run 1 mile in maybe just under 13 minutes, not killing myself, but breathing deeply.

Conclusion Number 1.* *So my running career had ended. But I did what Ted Haydon said and even educators say, I became a lifelong learner, with a lifelong interest in running, which is what it's really about for people, because everybody can't be a star and being a star is fleeting. But I hope you enjoyed my story so far and learned something and read the workout matrix at the back of the book. And some of you give me a call, and we'll work on some track workouts for you. Thank you.

Where New Yorkers run and I did in 1977. Around the Central Park Reservoir-one mile. For those who prefer urban landscapes.

My favorite running place, Palos Forest Preserve outside of Chicago

HERE'S THE OTHER STUFF- MY VIEWPOINTS

Comments on track, life, more Russia, USA economic issues and black and white athletes I knew

TRACK TODAY

About track today, I follow it. Somewhat. I watch how the runners compete. They're running great times. There's a lot of great runners. I'm disappointed at how widespread this doping has become. It's happening in the United States. It's a lot more than just the Russian Olympic team. They just got caught and did it more flagrantly most likely. Not everybody did, just some of them. And I'm sure it's widespread around the world. Track seems to have lost some of its aspects of glory and honor for some reason. Like a lot of things, the corporate ties have made it more like a machine, the athletes as well, it seems to me. And running for money. I don't begrudge them. I think it's good. But it just changes the whole notion of athletics. And to me, it's taken some of the essence, the spirit of it and debased it to kind of a commercial operation.

One thing I know is that the runners train extremely hard today, more distance and intensity than we did. And they are running faster. But I sometimes think they overdo it. It's interesting to note that our top USA 800-meter runner, coached by Lee Labadie, who is a few years younger than me and ran at Illinois in the early '70s, and was one of the few Big Ten athletes to break four minutes in the mile, (3:59) in those day prior to 1984. I saw some of Clayton Murphy's workouts on an internet video. They're sort of similar to mine in essence. At least this workout looked that way. There is a speed endurance emphasis. I don't think he's running really that much hard speed work. That's my best guess.

I recommend running pace endurance work with the emphasis more on endurance and strength then running real hard intense workouts in terms of anaerobic deficits (that means consuming more oxygen than you're breathing in). In the last 150 meters, you have to be able to go anaerobic and hold pace so you have to increase your total oxygen capacity to push off that anaerobic threshold where you begin to slow down and tie up. This requires repetitive interval workouts where you up your anaerobic threshold, increase aerobic capacity. I noticed he also runs evenly paced races, another sign of an

endurance trained athlete. Speed 800 meter runners tend to run the first 400 very fast, a split of 49-51 rather that 52-53. Another even split strength runner was the great US Olympic athlete from Oregon Nick Symmonds.

Track and Field Training Camps

I've talked about shoe companies a little before, but I just want to say again what I think the major shoe companies should do, and I think what I've mentioned in there, is create training camps around the country, maybe four, where they train not only the elite Olympic athletes, but the hopefuls and determined who might be ranked fourth or fifth through twentieth in their particular event. And anybody can go, and it's all paid for. They get room and board. And they are given some sort of part-time job in the area that's compatible with training and have financial support to send them to meets and pay for the fees and travel expenses. That's what I think should be done. I think we're lacking that. It would just be a good thing to do for sportsmanship, and potentially creating a deeper and more diverse Olympic team. You know, everything doesn't have to come down to the bottom line, does it? The problem we have, I think, in this country is that people at the top, the celebrities, the sports stars, the chief executive officers, the elites get paid enormous amounts of money, and most everybody else is falling behind, which tends to be ignored. I think we need a larger sense of the public good. Track would help by having these training facilities. My goodness, we could afford them with the profits the shoe companies make, and the companies who provide apparel for athletes, as well as state and federal governments. Let's get on board here. Let's start looking at the bigger picture. And it would be great, someone could come out of college, and they had promise as a runner, but they weren't finishing in the top three or four in the National meet. But they were still good. They may have even qualified and got eliminated. And they could say, "I want to really give it a year. I'm going to go to this training camp," wherever it might be. Houston, Los Angeles, Oregon, Chicago, Florida. And spend a year, not have to go to college, not have to get a job, but train and see what develops. And it doesn't matter if they don't become Olympic athletes. It's just that we do something for the sport. Come on people, let's get a little serious here. Other companies with money could also chip in. How about Apple, Amazon, Facebook, Tweeter, Microsoft, and the major banks?

Black and White Athletes I knew (and some I wish I had)

I remember my experiences, as I said earlier, of coming from the South Side. Running track, I became associated with black athletes, men and women, but where I lived then there were no blacks in that Polish neighborhood. It was white ethnic, Slavic. And then I moved to Evergreen Park, which was all white, and it stayed that way for years. But I remember, a wonderful African-American man named Art McClendon, who admired me and my running ability. He was 50-something, I guess, when I was about 19. He was a runner. He used to go out there and run these long distance races. And I really remember him and I running a Jackson Park six-mile run. He plodded along near the back. He treated me very nicely. And it was great to meet a successful black lawyer, very professional, had an office downtown. And he had a wonderful wife. And I take my hat off to you Art. I think about you fondly.

I also remember the Mayor Daley Youth Foundation, this fantastic track club of black women. Joe Robichaux was the coach. He was a heavy guy. He always wore a suit with a hat, and he chomped on a cigar. He was just the most amazing character. I can remember when the women athletes were running relays about 50 team members really getting excited up in the wooden stands at The University of Chicago. They would pound their feet and clap in rhythm. It was just a fantastic thing to see. My friends who weren't involved in track and lived back in Evergreen Park didn't get to share this type of wonderful culture.

I remember I was introduced to Dick Gregory once, the comedian and civil rights activist by Ted Haydon. And that was quite a thrill.

I also want to talk about the 1968 Olympics. Tommy Smith and John Carlos, when they got their Olympic medals for the 200 meters, raised their right hands in a fist with a black leather glove on. It created a real uproar. But I have to admire them because black people were treated terribly despite the 1964 Civil Rights Act. And they were making a point that black athletes shouldn't be used by a country to further its glory when the average black person was being mistreated. And an object of racial prejudice. They didn't lose their medals, but the Olympic committee sent them back to the US immediately. But Ted Haydon, who was an assistant coach on that Olympic team, was the only coach who congratulated them and told them they were very courageous and patted them on the back and told them to be proud of themselves. I agree.

There was also another character, the DePaul University coach Don Amadei, who later became coach of the Northwestern University Wildcats. Don was probably in his 40s then. He was a former Chicago boxer, prize fighter. And he yelled and screamed at his athletes. He smoked a pipe. But he was always training his athletes very hard (too hard for me). He was quite a character to see him out there. He also had an intellectual side. He was a specialist in Egypt. And I just want to say, Don, you made the Chicago sports scene a lot more colorful.

I want to mention one other little trip I took. And this is part of the adventure after I had graduated from high school in 1965, the NCAA track meet in 1966 was at Indiana University about 200 miles south. So what I did, with my parents' permission of course, I went down to Midway Airport. And we didn't live far from there. And I hopped a plane to Indianapolis and got off there. I knew Dick Schurke, who had coached me some, was down there. I was going to try to find him in one of the dorms. There were hundreds of athletes there. So I didn't know what to do. I had a little suitcase. And I just went out to the edge of the Indianapolis airport, and a truck driver picked me and drove me the 70 miles from Indianapolis to Indiana University in the town of Bloomington, Indiana. A beautiful place. And I spent three magnificent days there, watching the NCAA meet, just fascinated and in awe, marveling at these athletes, just thinking they're so fantastic, admiring them, hoping to be like them. I remember one night it was an extremely hot humid Indiana summer. The sun had just set. The air was still. I ran out in the farmland along a paved road four miles, just cruising with the flow, connected, in the "ZONE". And when I came back I was just so exhausted. But it was such a great feeling to feel the texture of the air and that Indiana corn, and the feeling of being part of the environment. I remember it well. And all the friendly Hoosiers down there

I remember Dick King, the quiet and older distance runner, who barely lifted his feet off the ground. Age then 50? He went to races far and wide and was a hermit of sorts. His pastime, his entire life, revolved around running, slow and alone. Another University of Chicago Track Club character. And Ken Young who ran a Marathon on the UCTC indoor track all by himself!! Unbelievable. 210 laps. Also Pat Palmer, Professor Emeritus of Astrophysics at The University of Chicago, former president of the University of Chicago Track Club and long distance runner.

This is just a smattering of the things that track brought to me. It brought me great adventures, and adventures other people didn't have. And it just wasn't the running and the races. It was all the other side things and the interesting people I met and seeing new areas and new ethnic groups. I remember one summer with the University of Chicago Track Club, I was probably 17 or 18, in the middle of July, we took a train to Buffalo, New York, overnight. We called it the milk train (that's because it stopped so much and was so slow). And up at Buffalo, there was a massive all day major East Coast AAU relays meet. We brought about 15 athletes, ran in all kinds of relays. I may have still been in high school, or maybe I had just gotten into college. But it's another one of those really interesting things that doesn't ordinarily happy to somebody.

Muhammad Ali

Hats off to a tremendous boxer and courageous person. What a classy and graceful boxer. He took a stand against the Vietnam War military draft and refused to be inducted into the US Army, subsequently lost his boxing title for over 3 years, and risked a prison sentence, showed a high commitment to ideals beyond boxing. He said "I ain't going to Vietnam to fight other people of color for any war when my real fight is here in the USA for racial justice". What a person!

Emil Zatopek

A great runner from the early 1950s from Czechoslovakia, who was known for his hard workouts and extremely good distance running times, putting out tremendous efforts. The point is he, like me, ran in the snow. And also in combat boots. Me in air force flight boots and in snow. Training to get an extra edge. And it was interesting -- I didn't know about this at the time when I was in high school. But we thought alike. I just find that interesting. Don't you, folks? What do you think about that? He also was somewhat of a dissident or a contrary in Czechoslovakia in the 1960s and 1970s. I kind of am too. I'm sort of a champion of the working man or the downtrodden. Always feeling the people at the top need to be kept in check. All right.

Billy Mills

The great Lakota Sioux Indian who grew up in poverty on the Pine Ridge Indian Reservation. He won the Olympic Gold Medal in the 1964 Olympics with a stunning come from behind victory passing the Great distance runner Ron Clarke of Australia. Today a successful business who supports the Lakota through his organization Running Strong for Indian Youth. A wonderful person.

Paavo Nurmi-Finland runner

Known as the Flying Finn he was the top distance runner in the world in the 1920's and set several world records. He was an influence on me. He also trained in heavy army combat boots and raced at a steady fast pace, utilizing timed interval training. He trained in the cold winter air, running through forests and rural roads, developing toughness.

Frank Shorter-Gold Medal Marathon

When I saw Frank leading the marathon in 1972 I immediately was impressed by how smooth he was running with confidence, just pouring it on. He was well trained but also running from his inner self and in the "ZONE" This is what I mean by "flow" I knew Frank slightly and recently exchanged letters with him. He did a lot for American distance running and was the last US runner to be highly successful in the Olympic Marathon. He also finished 2nd in 1976, the Silver Medal.

HENRY RONO WORLD RECORD KENYAN AND US CITIZEN

An interesting thing has happened while I'm here living in Albuquerque. Just last summer, 2016 I've made friends with Henry Rono, who was the world premier distant runner between 1976-80. In '78, he was named best athlete in the world. He set four world records in 81 days in the 3,000-meter, 5,000m, the steeplechase, and the 10,000m on the track. He lives here. He's trying to get something going in track. He works as a skycap at the airport. He lives a very simple life, and it's a hard job. And he does these tremendous workouts for himself on the weekends where he spends two to three hours walking, jogging, riding his bike, swimming in the pool, being in the sauna, the whirlpool. It's just amazing. And I know Henry has a dream to coach and he's had a difficult time of it because he doesn't really know exactly how to go about it, to sponsor some athletes and help them train. He's worked at the high schools here a few times, but he'd be willing to work anywhere nationally or internationally where he could coach distance runners. So I hope he gets that dream. It's hard to find the market. And I'm sure it's out there somewhere. Maybe somebody reading this knows it can help him. And he has a Facebook page, and I can put you in touch with him. To me it's an honor to be around this great Kenyan, who had a big struggle in his life, as well as great success, and just to know him. I consider that an honor. He also hopes to establish a running camp in Albuquerque.

I am always amazed at how graceful and natural Kenyans run. They also emphasize distance and repeat comfortable interval workouts rather than intense speed work.

SOUTH SIDE OF CHICAGO

What I remember is we used to play baseball when I was eight, nine, 10 years old at Cornell Park right in the Back of the Yards. There was a big Chicago Hot Dog place there, still is. Love them Chicago Dogs. We used to round up seven or eight of us on Saturday mornings and go down there and play baseball all afternoon. Sometimes four and four against each other, or we'd team up and find another team from another neighborhood and have a seven-inning game, six on a side. It was really fantastic. And the interesting part, you know, I grew up right in the heart of the Back of the Yards, which I'm really proud of that when I think about my South Side Chicago upbringing. And that's where my roots are. And I look very fondly back towards those days. In fact, I've driven past my old house a few times here in recent years, and the neighborhood has changed, but my block is in good shape. And we have some new immigrants coming in. But I really feel there is something special and unique about that South Side of Chicago. That's maybe why I'm a White Sox fan today, even though I always liked the Cubs, the Yankees. I've become a Sox fan, and I also cheer for those Yankees. And every time I go to Chicago in summertime, I try to get a game in. I sit on the third base line about the first, second or third row, about half way out in the outfield in the sun. Took my son Blaine, 28, there this summer. We sat in the first row, about where the outfielder stands. It was just fantastic. Really a lot of fun. And good White Sox food.

The downside is that not far from where I lived, just about 2 miles west of The University of Chicago, the neighborhood almost looks semi-rural, so many homes are missing with vacant yards all over the place. Weeds are growing high. Some buildings are boarded up with holes in the side. Existing occupied homes are scattered about. Hard to believe it's urban Chicago. This would be a good place for the Obama Presidential Museum and Library, since the President was a community organizer and this blighted area could use that economic development that he encouraged and thought necessary for the distressed inner-city black people. But no museum Presidential library in my Jackson Park. Construction has just begun.

When I was growing up, we had all these adventures. We'd break the boundaries of our neighborhood where we were supposed to stay, and venture into new areas, like Sherman Park, a big place full of bushes with trails and stone bridges over a large circular lagoon. It spurred our imaginations. We'd go on these half-a-day walking or bicycle excursions into exploring new areas, new parks, and it was quite exciting. And I think that had something to do with my success later in life. This determination to

discover new areas and new things and frontiers about yourself. I remember the little stores, each street corner in the old neighborhood would have a little store where they sold bread (25 cents a loaf for good Wonder or Butternut white bread and popsicles for 7 cents). I'd go there for ice cream bars and gum. And it was just the greatest fun in the world. We'd get baseball cards with that really delicious and wonderful smelling bubble gum. These little corner stores in this part, were quite ethnic Polish. There also were corner taverns all over. Now if I was older I'd probably been in there. But it's nice, the working man could come home, just walk, not drive down to the corner, meet his friends, talk to the bartender, have a little social time by himself. And sometimes probably bring the wife as well. I think it was a nice way to live. Also all summer long there were church carnivals, what a treat. The tilt-a whirl, little boats in water going in circles, throwing baseballs at metal milk bottles, and cotton candy. Wow.

Chicago Catholic Church Summer Neighborhood Carnival

I lived in a total Catholic neighborhood. It was Slavic, mostly Polish, some Ukrainian, and a few other ethnicities thrown in. And everybody was Catholic. So on Wednesday at 2:00 p.m., Fulton Elementary School practically closed down, almost the entire student body was Catholic and walked about three blocks past my house to St. Basil's Catholic Church.

In 1954 there was even a school where all the students spoke Polish, not English.

Roman Catholic cathedral built in 1922-awesome

We actually took an hour out of public school time to go to the parochial school, St. Basil's, and we had catechism lessons, you know, where they taught us about the Catholic Church and religion, which later became on Sunday mornings. But it's a totally amazing event. I bet you can't even believe it. There also was still a grammar school there where they spoke only Polish not too far from where I lived.

Me on right, and friends, Malcolm far left, Carl middle, Chicago 1955

I also remember the smell of burning leaves. We'd rake the leaves, put them in big piles on the curb. We had kind of narrow paved streets, and we would burn those leaves. And they smelled so wonderful with the smoke in the air, the wafting of the smoke and the great natural odor. Of course, you don't have that today. It's against the law. But it was part of the texture of growing up in those days, and I'll never forget it.

I also remember my mother taking me to Jackson Park Beach. It was around 59th and the lake, right by the Museum of Science and Industry, past The University of Chicago. And the funny thing is, you know, I loved going to that beach, but it was an integrated beach with blacks and whites, very unusual in those days. And I always wound up playing with a young black boy, at whatever age I was, four, five, six. And then my mother became friends with the child's mother. And so it was just a natural human relationship without any barriers of prejudice and fears and all those kind of awful things. It shows we're all the same. We all can live together.

I also remember the huge U-505 captured German WWII submarine being pulled over Lake Shore Drive to the Museum of Science and Industry. Took a few months. I was awestruck.

U-505 German WWII captured submarine being hauled across beach into Museum 1952 and me below

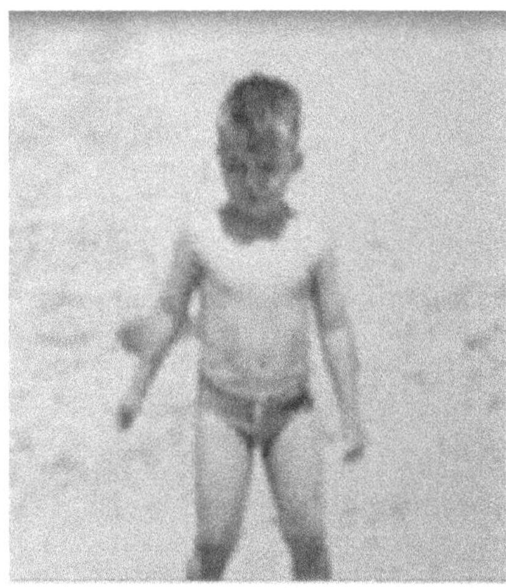

Above: Me at Jackson Park 59th St. Beach 1951. Below: Age 6 or 7 ready to go.

Pretty snazzy dresser.

South Side Bungalow just like my home

Museum of Science & Industry-a wonderful place

Me 1952 making a sand harbor at Jackson Park 59th St. Beach

Me 2018 age 71 eating at Tom's Steak House since 1952 near Chicago. Great steaks and old-fashioned salad dressings homemade. Typical Chicago Steakhouse in Melrose Park.

MY KIDS

I have two beautiful children, Kate age 44, Blaine age 29. Both were great runners. It seems as if this is an inherited, genetic quality. And we're all built kind of the same way. Kate has a lot of endurance. Blaine has a tremendous amount of natural endurance with pretty good speed. It's like we're all cut from the same tree. Very interesting, isn't it? So my daughter didn't really compete in track. But interestingly enough, when she was probably in 8th grade, she ran a one-mile race in Lake Forest, Illinois. One of those all-comers meets where they have a 5K and everything else. And she hadn't really trained. She just ran it and won the race with other young kids mostly, who were under the age of, oh, 14, and some adults, who weren't good runners. And I was totally amazed. I still have that trophy. My son really became a great high school runner starting in junior high. I was amazed he was running track in the 7th and 8th grade. And he was very good. First of all, he ran cross-country. And he was the best cross-country runner. And then in track that's when he started his racing. He ran the 400 meters. He was one of the best kids locally. Then believe it or not in 8th grade, he went to the unofficial youth State Meet in Peoria, Illinois, for kids his age, 12, 13, 14 year olds, who hadn't quite gotten to high school. And he ran the 400m, and he finished second or third of the entire state. He ran a great time for a kid that age. His time was around 54. That's really quite outstanding. And his coach trained him, but not real hard. I was really enthusiastic and impressed. That was about 2003. Then he went to Lake Forest High School and went out for track and cross-country and was the best runner on the team. In cross-country, he ran really hard. He wasn't the best cross-country runner, but he was probably the third or fourth best just like me, maybe a little better. And the coach was an extremely hard trainer. I thought he trained him too hard. But they won the Conference Championship, did well. And then in track, again, it was very hard training. I tried to influence the coach, but to no avail. I was actually meddling, but I was worried about my son's outcome. He had a few injuries now and then. But overall, he ran some very hard workouts, sometimes as much as 16 or 20 x 200m. And he became a great 440 and 880-yard runner. During his Senior year at the Conference Championship he ran a 49.1 and a 48.4 400-meter split on a mile relay at the District Meet. In the 800 he ran 1:54 to 1:56 several times, anchoring their 4x800 meter relay. It was one of the best relay teams in the state. I truly believe if he had only run the 800 at the State Meet his senior year in 2007 at Eastern Illinois University, he would've run about a 1:53 and finished second, I am convinced. The winner ran 1:52. And he would've had a full track scholarship to numerous schools in the Midwest. I was disappointed that didn't happen. His teammates convinced him to go out more slowly in the relay which left him in the middle of the pack. He was always a front

runner. Blaine would go out very fast and hang on, using his natural strength and hard interval training. He had a hard time running in the crowded pack around the other runners, ran slower, and his team did not make the finals. He was heartbroken. A lesson learned, do not change your running tactics and style. Why he didn't ask me I can't figure. I would have told him to run like you did all season, go out fast, stay out of trouble in the pack, and hang on. Too bad. After high school he went on. He trained with the Chicago Track Club for a while when he was 19. And he started running really well. He won a large invitational meet at Carthage College indoors, ran about a 1:56. But then he just lost interest. He got slightly injured. So he faded from his collegiate track career. I was rather disappointed to say the least. I tried to get him into Illinois State and then the University of Iowa. Larry Wieczorek, the great Big Ten distance runner, and the coach said he'd take him as a walk-on. Blaine had just lost interest. And he had some problems with his legs. Blaine still holds the school 440 yard

record at Lake Forest High School. And here, how many years later is it? Ten years later. He's very proud of that. And I gave him a trophy and some other things I made up for him. He created his own scrapbook of running. I still have all his newspaper articles. He was somewhat famous in that Chicago area North Suburban Conference.

The good thing is they developed a lifelong interest and appreciation of being fit. They both lifted weights and still work out on different exercise programs and ran on and off over the years. And that's one of the attributes of becoming interested in running. It's just like running and reading, lifelong commitments and improvements. Kate ran in some 5Ks, 10Ks, a few years ago when she was about 39 and did rather well. I was very impressed. She was doing a lot of running. But then she had a problem with her hip, her back, and couldn't keep it up. Such is life. My daughter Kate today is a successful businessperson with a middle management job. She is also raising a beautiful family. She has a husband and three children, my grandchildren. Are ages six to nine. I'm very happy for her. My son is a marketing and sales consultant for a large Swedish company involved in high tech supply management. They both work in the Chicago Metropolitan area. He's doing a bang up job creating a Facebook page for this book and helping me market it.

So I'm very happy for them.

Grandchildren—can't forget about them. John, age 6, smart as a whip, advanced in math, and a baseball player. He won't take any bull from me. Brooke, age 9, becoming a great swimmer, student, and young lady. And Sarah, Brooke's twin sister. She is a great soccer player, loves math and science, and already want to do something in environmental research. Yeah!!!! They call me grandpops, after my loving grandpops.

LET'S TRY AND LEAVE THE WORLD IN ONE PIECE FOR THEM.

I am releasing another book soon that I wrote as part of this book titled ANIMALS, INDIANS AND SPIRITS. It is about my experiences on the Pine Ridge Indian Reservation in southwest South Dakota from 1996-2008. I was a college teacher there from 2006-2009 at Oglala Lakota College. It was truly a fascinating experience. I helped the people and the Lakota Sioux helped me. I was deeply immersed in their culture. I also lived on the Navajo Reservation for one year. Watch the movie Thunderheart. The next several pages are mostly pictures taken by me of magnificent animals at Pine Ridge. A spirit man told me they consider buffalo and wolves to be their brothers.

ANIMALS

My grandkids and their great black dog, <u>Burma,</u> who I accompany on numerous walks when I visit. She is very insistent about this twice a day. We have gotten to know each other rather well over 8 years.

BURMA AND ME

SNUGLY MY DOG DACHSHUND CURIOUS LOVING MISCHIVEOUS-SIMILAR TO A WOLF

Painted by Elton Three Starts-Oglala Lakota

SNUGLY-Descendent of Wolves

WOLF

WOLF SPIRIT-painted by Elton Three Stars-Oglala Lakota

Do you feel the spirit of the wolf looking inside you?

READERS NOTES: What do you know about wolves? And what do you think about them?

MAGNIFICENT WOLF

BEAUTIFUL ROMAN CATHOLIC CATHERDRAL BUILT 1922

READERS NOTES:

Is there any difference between the magnificent spirit of one of nature's beautiful intelligent social animals and our worship of unseen spirits and saints in a church?

Buffalo Pine Ridge Indian Reservation

Very smart animals suited for the American Great Plains, unlike cattle that were imported from Scotland and England.

I speak about the <u>wolves</u>. Pure ignorance and unconscionable cruelty by sports hunters and ranchers. Wolves belong, they are social animals, never attacked a person unless in captivity and teased. My friend had two huge wolfdogs at home and I stood next to them in the kitchen. Just

gigantic, shoulders at my hips. I was very nervous and wary. Wolves Belong.

TATONKA-2500 POUNDS

Elton 3 Stars relaxing in my Lazy Boy chair. He painted the pictures of the wolf and my 2 dogs in this book. They are lifelike, uncanny, you see and feel their souls, their essence.

PICTURE OF ME 2002 BLACK HILLS LONG HAIR

-

The Lakota Oyate [People] gave me the name TWO DOGS because my 2 dogs were always with me.

<u>Conclusion. #2:</u> **Well, it's been a long journey in this book for me, taking me back in the past to 50 years ago. I hope you've enjoyed it. There are some other things, you know, I've not only discussed running. I've discussed how I felt about it and touched on other issues that I think are important, that hopefully will get a wide audience. I hope you learned about me a little and got a little extra insight into some ideas, whether you agree about them or not doesn't matter. It's just something for you to think about. That's why I use the phrase in the book title *"and Other Stuff". My Ten Years as a Middle-Distance Runner and Other Stuff.* So I hope you have enjoyed it. More to come now.**

<u>Next is a brief section about Russia. And I just want to say this. It also pertains to China. I discuss this in detail in my upcoming book.</u>

There are two things you need to understand about Russia.

1. **It always was an empire and now again is rising to become one after a chaotic transition in the 1990's. It, like most empires, exerts influence around its borders that usually have long historical ties. Think Ukraine, Belarus, Georgia, and the Asian countries like Kazakhstan and Uzbekistan. The US exerts its influence in Central and South America.**
   It has no tradition of western European style democracy and is a centralized strong state. Most of the population is satisfied with their political system.
2. **Russia has been invaded numerous times and lost heavily, 30 million people in WWII alone. It has a wary and defensive attitude towards Europe, NATO, and the USA. This influences their foreign and military policy. Their military is mostly defensive contained around its borders and not stretched all over the world like the USA. The world has three empires, China, Russia, and the USA (the new kid on the block). All competing for influence.**

RUSSIA-the BEAR

Kremlin at Night

RUSSIA is BIG

READERS NOTES: How many miles across is Russia? Number of People? Miles north to south? Does this large size make it more difficult to govern?

Do you consider Russia to be an enemy of the United States? Explain your reasons.

WESTERN RUSSIAN EMPIRE 1914 Includes Poland, Ukraine, Baltics

KREMLIN RUSSIAN GOVERNMENT

I speak about Russia again because I know something about it. It interests me. I was there in 1968 as a student at Northwestern University with the Russian department. We studied the Russian language and the culture and met all kinds of interesting people. I was there for five weeks in Leningrad and Moscow. I was an idealistic young man, somewhat intellectual, a history and political science major. So I really was interested in seeing another country, particularly one that was considered our enemy. Frankly folks, as I have already said, they weren't my enemy, and they still aren't. There may be government-to-government issues. But I don't believe in having enemies unless it's something clearly extremely threatening and immediate. I recently polled my economics class college students about foreign enemies. Out of 28 students, only 1 student considered Russia an enemy, 2 chose China, and 4 Iran. And

there was some overlap. Another young 26-year-old said she didn't get what all this stuff was about the US having enemies. She didn't think so. So these Millennials are hope for the future. They don't have "existential enemies" like our US leaders and intellectuals, and the Neocons, the Deep State concept. The US and Russia just became afraid of each other due to certain ideological circumstances in the 1930s and 1940s and Stalin's purge of Russia and Ukraine. But Russians were and are a very kind people, and I enjoyed seeing how the Communists and Russian culture interacted with each other. I was in Red Square. It's a glorious, powerful place that goes back to past 1500. The Kremlin, which means fortress, is the center of the government. As I have said, and I'll repeat myself. I stood in front of Vladimir Lenin, the founder of the Bolshevik Russian Party in 1917, in his tomb, encased in a plastic bubble casket. You can see him. I stood two feet from him. I slouched, as Americans do with my hand in my pocket and a Russian soldier grunted something at me, yanked my arm out of my pocket and pulled it straight down and told me to be respectful. And that just said a lot to me. I remember another time I met a Russian young economics graduate student, who was probably two years older than me, about 23. We were talking about economics, capitalism, communism. And I was just curious. But what he said is, "We just believe our system, that means the Marxism/Communism state planning type of economy, in the long run will prove itself superior to yours. And yours will diminish." And exactly the opposite happened. But his commitment impressed me because it's interesting to see somebody who believes wholeheartedly and sincerely in something that's just the opposite of your own culture and economy. So we have to be aware of other people's attitudes. And their differences are just as valid, as long as they don't cause any direct harm to us. Read my next book about the conflict between the USA, Russia, and China and why the USA cannot win any regional military war against them despite overwhelming military power.

Washington Monument

THE UNITED STATES ECONOMY

Another topic I just want to mention here is the economy, the US economy, the world economy, and I have talked about it in this book as The Surge. My next book will discuss current US economic issues in detail over 100 pages. I'm an economics instructor, professor, and I know something of what I'm talking about in terms of general economic trends. I'm not going to talk about it all. But one thing we have to think about regardless of our philosophy and our leaders' philosophy towards economics, politically and socially, is we need a plan, a bipartisan plan to create an economy that has long-term sustainability -- and I use that word "sustainability"-- of economic growth with fairness and opportunity. This economy shouldn't be going up and down like a yo-yo based on quick changing expedient policies about interest rate targets and government spending and taxation. And when I say sustainable it doesn't just mean growth, it means good growth. Growth in national defense, in healthcare for sickness, for police is not good growth because those are social problems that need to be fixed by society that cost money that needs to be used for other priorities. But these institutions do need funding to solve these problems for fixing negative things: crime, disease, war, that we need less of. We need growth to build the society, human capital, physical capital, infrastructure, financial support for the needy, for seniors, education, parks and more. We need sustainable growth, and an economy that is providing good jobs for people that pay to sustain a middle class, which is most of the country frankly. It's like 70 percent of the country. And then add the people near the bottom who need help as well (50 million below the poverty level of $12,000 per person). And 80 million total people under $25,000. One-half of the US population has no-that's ZERO-- net worth. Really. Check it out. I'm one of them now. It is tough and comes with much anxiety. Do you know that the largest group in poverty is single women with children at 28% of the total number in poverty and that 50% of children are born into single parent households in the USA? A new normal.

GLOBALIZATION HEADWINDS & WAGE PRESSURE

Since 1992 almost two billion new people have entered the world labor pool as China, India, and the former Soviet Bloc of Eastern Europe opened their economies and trade barriers fell. This new large supply of labor has caused downward unrelenting pressure on wages.

Below: A few "socialist" public projects that saved and built the USA.

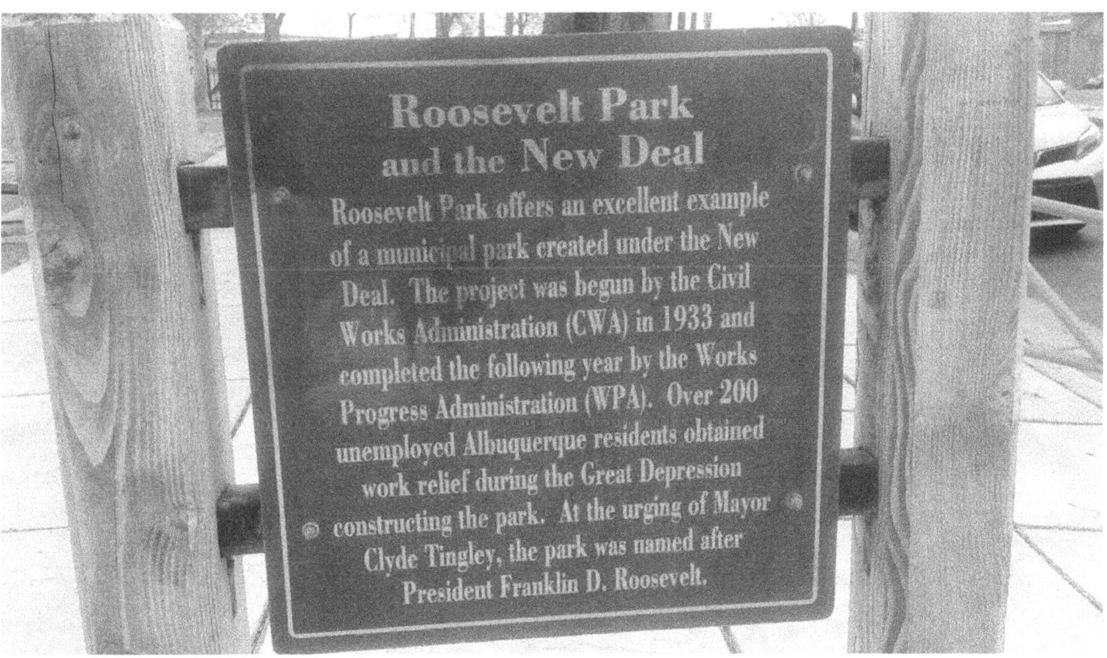

BUILT IN ALBUQUERQUE 1935 BY 200 UNEMPLOYED MEN. WORKS PROGRESS ADMINISTRATION NATIONAL PROGRAM. THE PARK IS STILL USED TODAY 83 YEARS LATER. IT HAS PROVIDED MUCH PUBLIC BENEFITS.

LUNCH TIME CCC or CIVILIAN CONSERVTION CORP. These 200 men did national soil, road, and forest restoration. Millions of trees were planted. The current National Park lodges were built. This is an example of tremendous public national benefits lasting until this day.

OLD GLORY USA FLAG

BROOKLYN BRIDGE-old infrastructure, still going strong. Where is the new infrastructure?

OTHER IMPORTANT STUFF

IMMIGRATION

On immigration, well, I live in New Mexico. And I don't know who is an illegal and who isn't. But we have had a lot of immigration. Forty-seven percent of the state is Hispanic. Forty percent Caucasian. Twelve percent American Indian, Native American. And one percent other, being Asian and African American. Actually, in the last seven years, immigration has slowed more or less. It's actually reversing itself. There's a little more flow back to Mexico as that economy has improved. Now I don't know if the illegals are the same way, but it probably is similar. And illegals do a lot of wonderful things in this country and support the economy. If there were no so-called illegals doing all of the gardening in the middle-class and upper-class suburbs and working on golf courses, there'd be a huge shortage of labor for those jobs. And I could probably get a $30 an hour summer job cutting grass! Green fees for golfers would rise. All this would really hit the budgets hard for middle-class people, who use all these people to get inexpensive gardening, grass mowing, fixing their flowers, doing odd jobs. Illegals also do a lot of work that is really undesirable, like working in packing plants where they kill chickens and cattle and gut them, and work in that really harsh environment and do a lot of the tough work. And they work on large corporate California farms. These farm owners are very concerned because migrant workers are leaving the workforce to return to Latin America for fear of being arrested and jailed causing labor shortages which will lead to higher food and wine prices or shortages. Heaven forbid! What will we do

with a shortage of your favorite California wine. They do a lot of the picking of vegetables and grapes in California. And I know there's nannies. Many are older women who take care of small children. Many are in Chicago, my home town. And they're from countries like Belize and Honduras. They're great Americans (just not citizens yet). They work for cash. They actually do pretty well, and are responsible. They have apartments. And they become a part of their families who employ them. It's a win-win. They help our American society. I know one. These "immigrants" also send huge amounts of money back to Mexico to help their families. After oil exports this is the largest source of foreign money. America gets low wage workers for rough jobs and Mexico gets financial help. A good trade.

READERS NOTES:

How would you solve the immigration issue? Be creative, fair, and compassionate.

Jackson Park in Chicago next to Lake Michigan

PRESIDENT OBAMA, AND HIS NEW PRESIDENTIAL MUSEUM, AND THE BEAUTIFUL OLYMPIC RUNNING TRACK WITH THE NFL CHICAGO BEARS FOOTBALL FIELD

Model of President Obama Museum

One thing I find disturbs me, it's unfortunate and I don't know if there is another option, then putting the Obama Museum in Jackson Park over the current, beautiful eight-lane Tartan track and football field put in by the Chicago Bears and the NFL. It was extremely expensive, and it's a great facility in a beautiful place, and serves the community and runners locally and also more distant places in Chicago too. There's a track program that's situated there, run by Rich Nayer, a friend of mine, called the Chicago

Track Club, [I am on the Board] which is different than the University of Chicago Track Club, [I am a lifetime member] which practices and has meets at Stagg Field. This is a spin-off of UCTC. Rich had a runner, a senior, age 40, who won a national outdoor USA Masters Championship! I was over there recently in the wintertime on a crispy 28-degree sunny Chicago day in about a foot of snow. I walked over to the track, and there was a path where several people had run around the inside lane in the snow cover. I'd been there in the summer. It's just a beautiful place. And it's bucolic. It's situated with Stony Island Ave. on one side and Washington Park Cornell Drive on the other. And it's just such a marvelous facility. There's a magic to it. It belongs there. I STARTED A "WALK/RUN FOR HUMANITY AND TED HAYDON" there, hoping it would catch on in 2013. Well we did this in December, temperature 44, not bad, just three of us, me, Rich Nayer, and Zeus Preckwinkle. It was great. We walked around Jackson Park on the sidewalk over to the beach, around the lagoon, back to the track, ran a lap, and finished behind the museum on the Clarence Darrow Bridge. We would have to divert some now from the Obama facility, but it could be done, about 2 miles. I was hoping it would pick up and have a few hundred of us good people there. Still can. I think the track has been underutilized. I said to Rich that the City of Chicago should sponsor some sort of regional track meet. We could invite some top athletes and talk to Rahm Emmanuel, the great Mayor of Chicago. But it's going to be destroyed. As of this printing it is starting to be torn up-is it too late to stop it? Probably. And it's really unfortunate. Moving it a block away won't do it, not the same. And the big new bulky museum will not have the magic of the Park, too imposing, too full of ideas about political issues, conflict. It will dominate the landscape. I don't think President Obama should be doing that. He should put that museum where he worked by The University of Chicago Law School and near the Woodlawn neighborhood adjacent to the south of the campus at 59th-60th Street. The Woodlawn community is a distressed crime ridden neighborhood trying to improve the quality of life for its residents, a neighborhood similar to where he did community organizing, (even though he did it in another part of the city). That would be his legacy. It is who President Obama is deep inside, committed to needy people. Not plunking it in the park because it's a good spot and it looks good. That is, you know, sort of contrary to what he professes to be his belief system. He's taking a part of the community. Then numerous international and outside visitors will make that part of the park busy and very congested. It is a large imposing structure out of character that clashes with the area. Reminds me of some Mesopotamian or ancient Babylonian temple. I just think it's not a good idea, and it should not happen. It will ruin the natural beauty and history of Jackson Park. More elites imposing their power. I want it out of there. It will gentrify the area and raise rents driving out the modest income people who live there now, essentially extending the Hyde Park higher

income area southward. Most of the new jobs will be modest wages and only provide the necessary income to offset the increased rents in the area or increased transportation costs. The net benefit will be zero. Except for a few highly paid managers and consultants. What do you think? I understand a new track will be built nearby, but that isn't necessarily the answer. Will it be as high of a quality, in such a picturesque place as the one now. The Museum will not solve the current neighborhood issues. A better location would be in Washington Park, 2 miles west and bordered by The University of Chicago and a low-income minority neighborhood.

The park is also distinctive and was built during the Columbian Exposition. I have run races there. It has a lagoon, winding streets, statues and a large fountain. Not bad. Should we restart the Walk for Humanity?

THE WOLVES

With the wolf Forest from Spirit Wolf Center

SOME OTHER REFLECTIONS

I hope you enjoyed this book. If you really read the workouts at the back here for those of you who are dedicated athletes, my e-mail is in there, send me an e-mail. We can talk. And maybe I'll help you train if you're so inclined. I made a speech at Northwestern University in 2011 when I was inducted into the Sports Hall of Fame. And one thing I remember is that a friend of mine, who was at my table, said I had a pretty emotional speech about track. To me, winning was life and death, and that sounds pretty awful. But it was fun in some ways, but in other ways it was more like a mission. I had the need to win. I had to win, perform well, and that propelled me. That propelled me to exceptional performance. I talked about it in this book. And it was that passion and commitment that nothing would stop me. It put a lot of stress on me and perhaps other people I knew, family members and friends. But it was certainly worth it.

I also have to mention that my education was superb. I was able to go to Northwestern University, a very prestigious and expensive private school that's in the Big Ten in Evanston, Illinois, on a track scholarship. Everything was paid for: room, board, tuition and books. Today that is over $65,000 per year! I was a kid from the South Side, could never have gotten in there, not enough money. But I did have the grades and the background to get admitted. I majored in history, got an A average in it. I loved it. Also, economics and political science. And that's when I developed my interests in international relations, the world, and national economic policies. At the age of 19, 20, it just hit me. And my politics and these interests haven't changed much since. I was awarded the Big 10 Medal of Honor and inducted into the Northwestern Athletic Hall of Fame.

Then I went on to get a Masters Degree in Business and Finance from The University of Chicago Graduate School of Business, something I very proud of. And of course, I ran down there with the University of Chicago Track Club and lived near there when I was a youth up to age ten. So it's all an interesting coincidence to be so close to an area where so many important things happened including my childhood days at the 59th Street Jackson Park beach and that whole community in essence, that extended community, the South Side, 55th to 47th Street, Damen Avenue to Ashland along Garfield Boulevard. I still wear University of Chicago and Northwestern University T-shirts and think about the

schools and visit them. I feel very honored. Thank you. This year I went to The University of Chicago Hospital for a meeting. Another continuing connection.

University of Chicago The Midway Pleasance

RUDY----The movie-see it. Very inspirational and a true story about a young man who aspires to get into Notre Dame University and play on their outstanding football team. He is from a working-class family in Joliet, Illinois, whose family works in the steel mills. Remember THE SURGE? His talent is limited but his heart and determination are unlimited.

NATIONAL USA LEADERS

<u>James Lovell-Astronaut Apollo 13</u>

In 1999 I drove a limousine in Chicago. I made many airport trips. It was a break after years of a high pressure banking/financial career. I liked it. And guess what? One time driving a passenger I noticed in the back seat was James Lovell going to visit his son in Lake Forest, Illinois. Wow! He was laconic, stoically quiet. I remember we were stuck at a long complex stoplight intersection of several roads. I watched him in the rearview mirror studying the traffic. He said "those stoplights need a reconfiguration". Here was an example of his engineering mind working away to solve a complex problem. I was impressed, and it certainly was indicative how an American hero steered the malfunctioning Apollo 13 spacecraft back to earth safely.

Martin Luther King Jr. and Malcolm X

Great brave African American leaders who advanced civil rights. I admire them. There is a community college in Chicago, named Malcolm X College.

The Kennedy Family

President John F Kennedy inspired me as he ushered in a new time of national service and US pride. Humorous and insightful, he led America towards a bright future. At one time after graduation from college, I considered joining the Peace Corp and a career in government service. The entire family is amazing with 100 members today, many active in politics and other leadership positions. I think they combine compassion for all people, are "liberal", fair minded, realistic, well educated, and committed to their beliefs. And coming from extreme wealth! I can only hope one of them arises into a major charismatic inspirational national leader. I think the Russia problem could be resolved realistically and peacefully and bridge the widening gap with that country. It needs to be done soon.

CENTRAL NEW MEXICO COMMUNITY COLLEGE OR CNM

I put this section in here because the college has been so good to me. Teaching economics has been one of the greatest experiences of my life and my favorite job. I love reading about the world economy and conveying that to my students who are mostly from modest socioeconomic backgrounds. Their eyes are opened to new realities and perspectives. Teaching is a respected honorable profession and I am grateful to be part of it. You should be so lucky. Sadly, large enrollment declines are reducing classes and forcing me to consider other employment options.

MY TRAINING NOW

As I mentioned earlier I have continued running. Last Fall, 2017, I did 77 days in a row of running and walking 30-50 minutes. BUT even an old timer can learn something and by being innovative and experimenting on myself I discovered just recently Swedish Speedplay/Fartlek training helped me break out of a slow training cycle. My legs didn't have enough push and power and I was running too slow for the effort. By putting in 75-150-meter intervals of high knee lift striding or at other times pushing hard off my feet leaning forward striding fast my running pace has picked up with a comfortable effort. There is also some additional brief cardiovascular stress anaerobic conditioning here too-hurts a little. I think I have taken at least 60 seconds, or 1 minute off my 2-mile running course time in about 3 weeks of training. So you see, I don't just talk, I experience it. I can help you, even if I was born 40-50 years before you. How about that! Lately, November 2018, I walk a mile, then run a mile or two at 12-13 minutes per mile 10 times a month. Feels good. Lost 15 pounds so I run faster and easier. Not bad for age 71.

New York City-Madison Square Garden

I remember in those University of Chicago Track Club trips to New York City to run in all the big meets indoors, which we won, we'd stay at, what I would call, an average, kind of non-descript hotel (the New Yorker) kitty-corner from the Madison Square Garden arena. After the meet, we would go to a place called Barney's, I believe, which is one of those long, wooden bars and steam tables characteristic of New York City, which we loved. We'd stay there until 1:00 in the morning, drinking some beer or some ginger ale and eating off the steam table, which they had everything under the sun: knockwurst, roast beef, sauerkraut, mashed potatoes, you name it. And these places stayed open late, it being Manhattan. And we'd talk about track, a lot of us and Ted, until we got tired and hit the sack.

I loved those indoor track meets in New York City. We also ran some other places, like Cleveland and Toronto. But they were, if you don't know them, they were 11-lap, wooden board tracks with a cork-like kind of bouncy surface. And they were tightly curved. Now with 11 laps you're really running fast around those turns. It seems like you're just tearing around. And inside the Garden of course, it seems like a small contained place, a highly charged enthusiastic informed crowd with electrical energy and buzz. All the officials wore a tuxedo. It was on national network TV. It felt like a sprint when you were running. It was so bouncy. And it was under the bright lights, and it had a real eclectic, exciting buzz to it, which doesn't exist in those new meets now, even if now held in a beautiful remodeled facility, in

New York City, called the Armory. The garden was packed with thousands of people. There weren't a bunch of empty seats. It was a major event. Those days are gone. I also enjoyed the Penn Relays. We would go there in April. There were great athletes there from all over. And it had a tremendous buzz too. We won the two-mile relay. It was exciting. We also ran in the Martin Luther King games in which we ran a good time about 7:20, but Kenya beat us and ran a 7:16. It was an honor to run against the Kenyans. And the fact that the Kenyan team won the Martin Luther King Two Mile Relay, one continent to another continent, said a lot to me about US race relations and Black history.

Six years later I lived in the east side of Manhattan at 353 East 83rd Street (at First Avenue).
On summer evenings at 6 PM I would ride my bike about 1 mile to the running path start next to the Museum of Metropolitan Art about 88th Street and Park Avenue. I locked it next to all the other bikes and ran 3 miles on the scenic horse bridle path around the Reservoir with many runners enjoying the evening. It was sublime. And around me were all the large New York office buildings, hotels, and apartments. I was young, impressionistic, and occasionally awestruck. I had come a long way from Evergreen Park in 1965. I also ran a 5K Sunday race in a slow moving mass of hundreds of runners-probably a few thousand moving in one mass through Central Park. I remember Saturday mornings about 9. I would glide around the Reservoir on the cinder bridal path, sometimes a horse and rider would come cantering by me. Afterwards I stopped at one of those New York City greasy spoon breakfast restaurants for a great meal of eggs, toast, bacon, sausages, orange juice, and steaming coffee. Life was good.

TED HAYDON-A TRACK & FIELD ICON- "TED"

TED HAYDON RENOWN COACH OF UCTC OR THE UNIVERSITY OF CHICAGO TRACK CLUB

I also want to pay a tribute to Ted Edward Haydon, a great man, an icon in the track world, who was coach at the University of Chicago Track Club and The University of Chicago Track team. I'm a lifetime member of that group. I suggest you read about it. He was a social worker initially in his career on the South Side of Chicago and graduated from The University of Chicago. He started the University of Chicago Track Club and worked at the university as a coach, starting in the mid-1950s. Ted was a great guy and is now a legend. He helped me a lot. He began his working life after getting a degree in sociology from The University of Chicago in the Chicago low income projects. Undoubtedly this had a major impact on his style of coaching and open mindedness. He was still coaching at age 73 when he died of a cerebral hemorrhage in 1986. He was coach of the USA Track Team that competed against Russia in 1975 and was inducted into the US Track Coachers Association Hall of Fame in 2001. He is a legend.

You can learn much more about him. Google "Ted Haydon Alibi List"" and click on "Ted-Haydon The University of Chicago Math Department".

There're three things I remember about Ted and me. When I was a senior in high school, (and I found out about this five years later), he told somebody when he was watching me practice, he said, "That's Ralph Schultz, he's going to be NCAA Champ someday." Well, about three years later I finished third. When I was at the NCAA my junior year at Berkeley, he was there at the meet watching. We had to run three hard 880s Thursday, Friday and Saturday, the semi-finals and the finals. He told me that in the morning, "Take an easy 15-minute jog to loosen up." This gets the lactic acid waste products flowing out of your system. And I did. And I ran well. Runners tend to stiffen up because they're tight from the prior days' effort. A blood stream waste product, lactic acid, builds in the muscles after hard running and inhibits running performance the next day if not flushed out. Have you seen runners who at the end of race slow down and tighten up like a rock? Well, probably too much lactic acid buildup and inadequate warmup. So he helped me in many ways. And I remember him fondly. He coached the University of Chicago Track Club and our two-mile relay team. He looked out for his people. And he's the one who helped me get a track scholarship at the University of Michigan, so I want to dedicate part of this book to Ted's memory. He was loved by many. And here's a funny story. 15 years later in 1987 I hadn't seen much of Ted. I showed up for the annual Riis Park Turkey Trot Race. I saw him and said, "Hi Ted, I have been training hard again". He took one long look at me, paused, and said, "For what Thanksgiving!!" (up 40 pounds). Hahahaha

Ted Sayings and Runner Alibis List-a few selections-

-"A good coach tries to correct your form, a great coach leaves you alone"

--One time in May of 1984 at the Stagg Relays, a runner finished last in his heat of the 800 meters in around 2:08. He came up to Ted and said, "I guess I got my butt kicked today." Ted replied, "No he would have had to be behind you to kick your butt".

--"Being a UCTC runner is a state of mind"

- Ate too much
- I was weak for lack of nourishment

- Too much competition
- No competition

- Girl friend unfriendly last night
- Girl friend too friendly last night

- I just didn't feel like running
- I felt great and that usually is a bad sign

Should I restart the Walk for Humanity and Ted Haydon I mentioned above? Will you join me? Jackson park is a beautiful historic place. E-mail me.

Me Today Summer 2018

<u>Conclusion #3</u>—THE LAST ONE

I hope you've enjoyed your journey with me in this book. I'm sure a lot of you track people are really surprised that it's really not a track book entirely, and I diverged on a lot of topics that I'm interested in. I wanted to get my ideas across because I think too often sometimes track people don't really discuss these sorts of things. And this may be my only chance to get those ideas across. I'm going 70 years old. I also have early stage bladder cancer. It's manageable. Well, I hope you discovered some new interesting ideas about the world and about running. To those of you aren't track buffs, you may have found the book interesting based on my story as a track guy growing up in Chicago and my ideas, as an American. And if you're from another country, you could get a viewpoint of a certain type of person and an insight into some American thought and ideas.

"If the United States continues looking for enemies it will cease to exist as a spiritually enlightened nation" [R. Schultz]

YOUR RUNNING TRAINING MATRIX

At the end of the book there is a matrix or chart of my workouts that I recommend. However, I would suggest you read the book, particularly the middle part that pertains to why these workouts are the way they are. I can summarize and say there's very little speed work. It's mostly rigorous pace endurance interval training, along with three to six mile runs of varying degrees of difficulty. Now remember a 1:48 800m is an interval workout of 4 times 200m at 27 seconds with a zero rest interval. A four-minute mile is an interval workout of 4 times 400m. at 60 seconds with a zero rest interval. If you keep that in mind, and you flow and relax when you run and train, you'll have the feel of what I'm telling you. The only speed workout for me, and which you'll have to try to fit it in somehow, is that about every weekend I ran on the mile relay or 4 x 400m relay. It was an all-out 440 (47-50 sec.) which gave me speed and strength. You might have to find a way to put that into your workouts. The other part of this is that the speed work is just running the last interval of a long 200 or 400 interval workout faster, pick it up a little, coast, but it's still fast. There's very little speed training, which some of you won't understand. But you have to do it my way if you want this to work. So feel free to call me, or my E-MAIL is NewMexcoach@gmail.com .We can discuss these workouts. I would like to also work

with you perhaps as your coach. And you can be anywhere in the world. it doesn't matter. We've got telephone, text messages, e-mails, Skype, you name it, and videos as well. So let's see what we can do. So please contact me if you need help. There are also athletes who are interested in getting involved and talking to other athletes. We can create a discussion board, and we can talk to each other and see each other's comments. And you can talk to athletes in other parts of the country or the world and compare track ideas and make some good friends as well. But thank you very much for reading this, and I wish you all well.

THE END

"

PICTURE SECTION

Left: COACH "MEGGIE" My Inspirtion

Above: Coach Megson giving encouragement. Below: Coach Ryan

Palos Forest Preserve Illinois 2017

Larry Wieczorek and me after 880 run 1969

Me at Pentagon Briefing Room 2016

Spanish interpreter track/field official tour guide

Final stretch 70 yards to go in 660. I ran 1:17.4 just ahead of Carl Frazier of Iowa.

Left: Me and my Navajo dogs.

My roommate Bob Hinshaw and I in Florida 1969

Start High School District Meet 1965

MONDAY, MAY 26, 1969

Schultz of N. U. Gets Big 10 Medal

Ralph Schultz of Evergreen Park, Northwestern's middle distance track star, was awarded the Big Ten medal for excellence in athletics and scholarship at the annual honors day ceremonies on the campus yesterday.

Schultz was Big Ten half mile champion as a sophomore and twice won the 1,000-yard indoor title. His winning time as a senior in the 1,000-yard run of 2:06 tied the world record.

Ray Forsthoffer of Cleveland, linebacker on the football team, was awarded the Walter K. Smart medal for accomplishments in athletics and scholarship. Forsthoffer is co-captain of the 1969 football team.

Greg Croft of Glenview, the leading pitcher on the baseball team, received the Thomas Coyne award for achievements in athletics and scholarship.

Bruce Hubbard of Arlington Heights, leading pass receiver on last year's football team, was awarded the Carleton and Bradford Pendleton memorial scholarship for athletic and scholastic achievement.

Me, Rich Christopher manager, Coach Ehrhart

Above: Roommate and Friend Bob Hinshaw

Below left: Coach Megson

Me in 2018 Official Los Angeles Dodgers Baseball Cap!

Coach Megson and my Mother at High School State Track Meet 1965

Family at Chicago lakefront. Blaine, Brooke, John, Sarah, Katie

Merrilyn-helper, friend

Me, Sarah, John, Brooke, the Grandchildren

Me and young students and teacher outside of Leningrad in 1968. This is about peace and the fact we are all one human race. I wonder what some of these little ones are doing today in Russia.

IS A MAJOR CULTURAL EXCHANGE OF EDUCATORS, STUDENTS, BUSINESS PEOPLE, AND GOVERNMENT OFFICIALS A GOOD IDEA TO PROMOTE BETTER UNDERSTANDING AND PEACEFUL RELATIONS WITH RUSSIA?

High School days-mother, me, coach at State Track Meet 1963

Below: me, mother in Arizona 1963 on edge of Navajo reservation traveling to California on vacation

Just me on Northwestern Track Team

My dogs, Starstream (above) and Snugly (below). The greatest Dachshunds I've ever known.

Above: Merrilyn Sweet   Below: Lope and Pandi our friends. Soon to have their own children's book "The Adventures of Pandi and Lope"

THREE OF THE ALL-TIME BEST USA AND WORLD SPRINTERS

Left: Tommie Smith World Record Olympic Champion 200 meters and John Carlos Silver Olympic Medal. Foreground left: Avery Brundage President NAAU & Olympics for USA. He sent Tommie and John back to the USA and banned them from any Olympic Games for life.

Right: Lee Evans World Record Holder and Olympic Champion 1968 400 meters

A TED HAYDON STORY: After Tommie Smith had been kicked off the Olympic team in Mexico, I (NOT ME, but a USA Olympic team athlete) saw him in the hotel lobby where I was staying. I went up to him, offered my hand and my congratulations. He did not take my hand, but asked, "What's that for man?". I said, "You won a gold medal, that's what it's for". He took my hand, saying, "That's what it's all about. Where are you from?". "Chicago" (I said). "Do you know Ted Haydon?" (Smith). "He's a good friend" (I said). "That explains it" (Tommie Smith)

THREE ALL TIME GREAT 800 METER RUNNERS

UPPER LEFT: YEVGENY ARZHANOV USSR/RUSSIA 1972 OLYMPIC SILVER MEDAL-UPPER RIGHT: PETER SNELL NEW ZEALAND OLYMPIC GOLD 1960 & 1964-BENEATH: RICK WOHLHUTER USA OLYMPIC BRONZE

Me after 3 mile walk run at local park route and the path, November 2

Altitude 5200 feet

GMAIL: NewMexcoach@gmail.com

RALPH SCHULTZ TRAINING MATRIX

	SUMMER 6/15-8/31	FALL CROSS-COUNTRY 9/1-11-15
MONDAY	4-7 MILE RUNS 3-4 DAYS WEEK cruise at varying pace @ scenic places	20 x 400 @ 68-75 sec.
TUESDAY	Run a few long hill runs Race in a few 5k's or track meets	6 mile paced run
WEDNESDAY		4 x 1 mile or 3 x 1.5 miles
THURSDAY		4-mile medium run
FRIDAY		easy race warmup
SATURDAY		Race <u>or</u> Time Trial or 45 min. hard fartlek
SUNDAY		3 -4-mile easy jog

CONSISTNCY IS IMPORTANT-DO NOT OVERTRAIN

LESS IS MORE-ANCIENT CHINESE PROVERB

RALPH SCHULTZ TRAINING MATRIX

	INDOOR SEASON 11/15-3/21	SPRING BASE REBUILD 3/22-4/10
MONDAY	8 X 400 @ 60-64, LAST @ 56-58- or 20 X 200 @ 30-32, LAST @ 27-28	2-3-weeks cross country training Alternate 20 x 400; 3 x 1200; 20 x 200; 4-5 mile runs & 45 min. fartlek with rest days
TUESDAY	3 MILE INDOOR RUN IN FLATS INCREASING PACE 7 MIN-6 MIN-5 MIN.	
WEDNESDAY	2400 (1.5 miles) TIME TRIAL or 2 x 1200 @ 3:04-3:12 - 600 jog rest or 4 x 800 @ 2:02-2:08 – 5 min jog rest These are run at race pace or slightly slower	
THURSDAY	SAME AS TUESDAY – 3 MILE INDOOR RUN	
FRIDAY	PRE-RACE WARMUP	
SATURDAY	RACE or TIME TRIAL or 45 min. hard fartlek*	
SUNDAY	EASY 3 MILE JOG-PICK UP FINAL 800 IF LOOSE	

*TRY TO RUN 4 X 400 RELAY SPLIT OR TIME TRIAL @ 95% each Saturday Indoors and Outdoors

Train & race at smooth steady pace-don't strain. Pre-major race week below is both indoors and outdoors.

RALPH SCHULTZ TRAINING MATRIX

	OUTDOOR SEASON 4/10-6/30 (TO 9/30 EUROPE) --In Europe extend indoor season training to May 1	PRE-MAJOR RACE WEEK** Conference, National, Invitational
MONDAY	1200 @ 3:00-3:10 then 3 x 400 @ 60-64 or Ladder 200 @ 29-30, 400 @ 60-64, 800 @ 2:00-2:10, 400 @ 56-60, 200 @ 27-30 Rest-jog distance run	6 x 200 @ 30-33 flush system of lactic acid
TUESDAY	3-mile continuous run 7-6-5	800 Race: 3 x 400 @ 55-53-57 with 400 jog rest (1:48 runner), medium-fast-slow 400--1500 Race: 1 x 400 @ 60-64, then 800 @ race pace, 2 easy 130's
WEDNESDAY	8-12 x 200 @ 27-30-medium effort 200 jog rest Vary pace descending to 27	3-mile continuous run 7-6-5 pace
THURSDAY	3-mile continuous run 7-6-5	pre-race warmup
FRIDAY	pre-race warmup	pre-race warmup-get loose
SATURDAY	Race, Time Trial or medium 4-mile run*	MAJOR RACE
SUNDAY	easy 3-mile jog, pick up last 800 to 70-80 pace	Easy jog or rest

**MAX WORKOUT 2-3 weeks PRIOR to MAJOR RACE--2 X 400 FAST 49-53 (800) or 800 fast 1:50-1:55 (1500-or-800) or 1 x 1200 @ 2:56-3:06 (1500). Easy running two days before and after workout.

HANDY WORKOUT CARD

Copy, cut, fold, put into wallet

HANDY WORKOUT CARD – RALPH SCHULTE

Summer
- EZ DISTANCE
- 4-7 mile RUNS
- 4 days / week

Fall XC
- 20 x 400
- 6 mile RUN
- 3 x 1½ mile OR 4 x 1 mile
- 4 mile RUN
- WARM UP
- RACE / Time TRIAL
- EZ 3-4 Mile RUN

INDOOR TRACK
- 20x200 or 8 x 400
- 3 miles 7-6-5
- 1½ mile Time Trial or 4x800 or 2x1200
- 3 miles 7-6-5
- WARM UP
- RACE / Time TRIAL / HARD FARTLEK
- 3-4 mile EZ RUN

OUTDOOR
- 8x400 or 2x1200
- 3 miles 7-6-5
- 8-12 x 200 (27-32) or 200-400-800-400-200
- MED. PACE
- 3 miles 7-6-5
- WARM UP
- RACE or Time TRIAL

BIG RACE WEEK
- M. 6x150 EZ 30-33
- T. 3x400 MED 56-54-58 or 400 [60-64] 800-RACE PACE 400 [60-64]
- W. 3 miles 7-6-5
- Th – WARM UP
- FRI – WARM UP or PRELIM
- SAT: RACE

Killer WORKOUTS
- 2x400 @ 95% 49-53 OR
- 400 – [60-64] 800 – FAST 1:50-55 400 – → MEDIUM 56-60

THE END

www.ingramcontent.com/pod-product-compliance
Ingram Content Group UK Ltd.
Pitfield, Milton Keynes, MK11 3LW, UK
UKHW051138260726
13967UKWH00010B/3123